GYPSET
STYLE

601 West 26th Street, 18th Floor
New York, NY 10001, USA
www.assouline.com

ISBN: 978 2 75940 396 7

10 9 8 7 6 5 4 3

Color Separation by Luc Alexis Chasleries
Printed in the United States

JULIA CHAPLIN

GYPSET
STYLE

ASSOULINE

CONTENTS

The interior of a Gypsy house in Madrid, 1999. Photo by Anne Mecke.

INTRODUCTION

My life in the gypstream

I first had the idea to write a book called *Gypset* while I was vacationing in a village on the Pacific coast of Mexico called Todos Santos, where I have spent winters since I was a teenager. It's mainly populated by farmers, fishermen, and a few expatriates. The roads are mostly dirt, and the main Friday-night activity is peeling around town in pickup trucks, blaring ranchero music, and drinking canned Tecate. The town also happens to have one of the best surf breaks on the coast, and one day when I was out at the beach La Pastora, I happened upon a mysterious couple. They own an amazing compound overlooking the surf break, with several palm-thatched huts, a riding stable that has been partly converted into a Gothic lair, and a painting studio that recalls Frida Kahlo by way of Topanga Canyon. Their freshwater swimming pool is shaded by banana leaves and desert flowers that they also use for irrigation. And by the beach, in a surf shack built of Palo de Arco branches, there is a fleet of surfboards, a canopy bed, and an acoustic guitar. Really, what more could a person want or need in life?

On any given day, strands of exotic-looking people, refugees from Hollywood or Parisian winters, are wandering the grounds in bikinis and sarongs, nibbling on coconuts, waxing surfboards, and snapping photographs of one another. The couple, Garth and Euva, are what I have come to define as Gypsetters. He is a novelist and legendary surfer, and she is an actress, fashion designer, and bon vivant who is famous in certain circles for her charm, style, and eccentric dinner parties. They are part of an elusive set of people who influence celebrities but are consciously hidden from the tabloids and mass media. This charismatic pair truly seem to have mastered the perfect life, where pleasure, travel, and livelihood all coexist in an eclectic style.

The author in Ditch Plains, Montauk, New York, 2007.

And so it was upon meeting Garth and Euva and discovering this pocket of energy in a little-known Mexican village that I began to think about the concept of Gypset. Gypset is an approach to life that fuses the wild and unconventional ethos of a gypsy with the sophistication and speed of the jet set. It's a lifestyle that crosses high and low—a surfer who is also a fashion designer, an artist who traded the go-go New York City art world for Bali's low-key tropical shores, a jewelry designer who would rather work out of a town in Mexico than in the über-chic Saint-Germain-des-Prés.

When I began writing about travel, I gravitated to the bohemian enclaves where the Gypsetters abound. Whenever I had the chance, I would pitch an assignment involving these special corners of the world. But it always seemed that some Gypsetter had already figured out to go there years earlier. I went to the hippie-chic Spanish isle of Ibiza and found ex-London fashion-philes camped out in old white-washed fincas and tepees. In Careyes, Mexico, I made new best friends with foreign accents from around the globe without ever learning their last names. In Máncora, Peru, I found an amazing pyramid-shaped surf shack overlooking three of the country's best breaks. In the summers I headed to Montauk, New York, and found a creative community hiding out at the end of gravel driveways. And in the little patch of land called José Ignacio that juts into the Atlantic Ocean north of Punta del Este in Uruguay, I noticed amazing architecture—modernist reworkings of traditional fishing huts with geometrically sculpted straw roofs. I discovered that over the course of the past decade an entire Gypset aesthetic had emerged. There was a group of people who, much like Garth and Euva in Todos Santos, were living a different type of dream. It was part pioneer, part artist, and part sheer indulgence.

My favorite thing about the Gypset lifestyle is that it's not about money, it's about a level of taste that can only be accessed from an approach to life that fuses high and low culture. Buying a luxury condo on an exclusive beach or checking into a five-star hotel is not in itself glamorous. Glamour—as confirmed when I stayed with Nathalie and Sophie Laurence Mignot, a pair of French sisters in Sayulita, Mexico—is about turning a rooftop into a supercool compound by painting the walls fuchsia, and firing up some votive candles for light. It's no coincidence that those who are defining the Gypset aesthetic are artists, fashion designers, photographers, musicians, and surfers whose work is based on their lifestyle and whose lifestyle is based on their work. Gypsetters are freethinkers who have made the choice to set themselves up far away—even if it's only for part of the year—proposing an alternative solution to life.

Some of my first memories of a nomadic lifestyle are from the back of a white Volkswagen van. My bohemian parents drove my sister and me from one far-flung adventure to the next, blaring the Grateful Dead and nibbling on pistachios. My father, a writer, insisted on moving every few years to end-of-the-road places that horrified my grandparents in Philadelphia: Key West, Todos Santos, and the Bahamas. Summers were spent on Cape Cod, in Chatham, in a dilapidated Victorian-era mansion

Clockwise: Learning to surf in Todos Santos, Mexico, at a rather fearsome break called La Pastora, 1997; in our backyard in Key West, Florida in the late 1970s at age 8 (on the left), with my older sister Diana, age 10; I found this bumper sticker on a rusty car in the surf town of Rincon, Puerto Rico. A perfect motto!; My family at our fabulously dilapidated summer house in Chatham, Cape Cod in the 1970s; Garth and Euva's surf shack in Todos Santos, Mexico; Diana (left) and me on our family sailboat, *The Ho Won*, Key West, 1981; watching the sunset in Todos Santos, Mexico. New Year's Eve, 2007.

belonging to so many members of my extended family that it was somehow completely forgotten. And there it was, sitting grand and practically abandoned on a cliff on the edge of town overlooking the ocean. (The rambling house made Grey Gardens look well kept.) My parents discovered the house and, being it was the seventies, turned it into a sort of seasonal commune stocked with friends and their families for the month of August. What a paradise!

When I moved to New York City after college, I began writing about trends and popular culture for newspapers and magazines. But inevitably I would begin to feel a cellular need to hit the road. I became obsessed with making a connection between the nomadic ethos of my youth and the fast-paced, highly creative world I was documenting in Manhattan. The central question I began to ask myself was, is it possible to have it both ways? The jet-set template didn't seem that exciting. I had hung out in this milieu on assignments and found the scene rather interchangeable and boring. I'll never forget going to Cartagena, Colombia, for New Year's, expecting to find who knows what, only to end up with a bunch of bankers from New York when the clock struck midnight.

It's much more satisfying to fuse leisure with creativity. I was always miffed by the "thank God it's Friday" ritual of blowing off steam at the end of the workweek. What happens if work and play are integrated? In this book each Gypsetter presents his or her own answer.

I should point out that the central difference between Gypsetters and the bohemians who preceded them is commerce. The new generation has a very different relationship to the idea of "selling out." The seventies showed us that dropping out, though it was an important mass statement, isn't the most effective use of a life. It's more effective to add your voice to the larger cultural dialogue.

In his pop-sociological book *Bobos in Paradise,* published in 2000, David Brooks theorizes that bohemian and bourgeois society melded in the 1990s and essentially became one—which he defines as "Bobo." (Bill Gates, a Harvard dropout who has built one of the most successful empires of his generation on progressive ideas is the archetypal Bobo, according to Brooks.) Gypsetters are a generation or two younger than Gates, or at least on another wavelength. They have grown up in an era when selling out was not really the issue. For them, the question is not whether to contribute; it's how to contribute on your own terms.

Ideally, Gypsetters, even those who spend part of their time in cities, have ferreted out a perfect perch, preferably in a town far enough from a major airport that those on tight schedules won't venture to visit. There they are free to think without all the cultural white noise. They travel often to gather ideas, seeking out the unpredictable and the unknown.

The Gypsetters featured in this book are people I regard with the utmost respect for having the courage to leave the city for a while to experiment with what I have come to imagine as the perfect life.

We were always moving, so this VW bus—our family caravan—felt like our one true home.
This picture was taken in Key West, in front of our conch-style house on William Street. (I'm up on the balcony.)

GYPSY ORIGINALS

Pioneers of the nomadic freelance lifestyle

"The Gypsy lifestyle is a perfect fantasy, and as we all know reality is often very different from the fiction." JOHN GALLIANO

There are no new ideas. Wanderlust and all of its glam ephemera—from layered skirts to tricked-out caravans—predate Western civilization itself. The Gypsies, or Roma, as they are known, left India around 800 CE. They walked through Persia, Turkey, and Greece, and arrived by foot in Europe five hundred years later. (What a stroll!) The various tribes dispersed around the continent, with clans ending up in Spain, France, Finland, and Russia, with the largest concentration in the Balkan countries.

Gypsies lived with their bags packed because, really, who knew when they might tire of a place and want to push off—or, as the case often was, when the place might tire of them? As an ethnic minority holding no territory of their own, Gypsies were often the first targets when intolerance arose. Their nomadic ways meant they were, by necessity, the original freelancers. Traditionally, Gypsy men worked as musicians and dancers. Gypsy women—deeply superstitious—read palms and tarot cards, cast charms, made spells, and sold fortunes at fairs and on the street. They were simultaneously an oppressed minority and mysterious strangers: Exotic, entertaining, and possibly from another world entirely. The Italian artist Caravaggio was intrigued, and in the sixteenth century immortalized one in his painting *The Fortune Teller*.

Gypsies naturally stood out from the medieval crowd; they had to. Fashion was their roadside billboard, a way of attracting attention to their wares and services. They were the forebears of street style, and because they invariably had just come from someplace else, their outfits were necessarily a mash-up of discarded threads collected during their travels. They subverted Renaissance notions of class: Whereas rich courtesans often wore upward of five costly layers and the lower classes had

A stack of mismatched colorful fabrics inside the home of a Madrid-based Gypsy family, 1999.

Opposite: Young Gypsy girls show off their field fashion in Spain, 1999. *This page:* Gypsies celebrating in the Spanish countryside, 1999; colorful skirt layers drying in the sun. Photos by Anne Menke. *Following pages:* A Gypsy man weaves a basket by his pink and green caravan in the middle of an encampment in France, 1959.

MT

to scrape together funds for one or two, the Gypsies just piled it all on, regardless of tailoring, quality, or etiquette. They layered laced vests, bodices, over-bodices, sorcerer's capes, floor-swishing tiered skirts, billowing blouses, and lots and lots of fringe. And then they added to the mix pretty much anything that they found along the way that was colorful and theatrical. "The ultimate flea market" is how Carla Sozzani, the owner of 10 Corso Como, the Milanese boutique that sells pricey Gypsy-inspired threads, once described the sartorial aesthetic. The Gypsies mastered the look long before university students discovered secondhand shops and hipsters began to fetishize "vintage."

Not surprisingly, the old-school Gypsy style has captivated the imaginations of generations of fashion designers: Yves Saint Laurent in the 1970s, Galliano in the 1990s, even the contemporary luxe wares of Gucci, Giorgio Armani, and Vivienne Westwood. All understand that the highest fashion looks simultaneously effortless and mischievous. "It's the total, unremitting freedom," designer Roberto Cavalli has said of his amped-up, Gypsy-inspired looks. "It's more than an aesthetic, it's a lifestyle; and it's boho to the max, exactly as I like it."

Of course, fashion has its price, and historically, for the Gypsies, it was especially high. Looking, acting, and indeed living differently often led to intense xenophobia and persecution in their host countries. Locals didn't take kindly to gangs of nomads showing up and camping on the outskirts of their communities, unwilling to assimilate. Unable to understand how the Gypsies could make a living without land or even seeming to work, the locals often persecuted them as thieves and witches. Gypsies suffered every horrible fate imaginable, including forced slavery, ethnic cleansing, and sterilization. The Nazis sent hundreds of thousands of them to concentration camps.

As it happens, some of the slurs and insults once meant to degrade and dehumanize the Gypsies have become compliments. The term "bohemian," for example, was first used in the nineteenth century by the French to describe Gypsies, who they mistakenly thought came from Bohemia, an area in central Europe that was considered backward and uncivilized. After a time it became fashionable for artists to shack up in the low-rent Parisian neighborhoods where Gypsies lived, so the derogatory label was extended to generations of creatives.

In Spain, *los gitanos,* as Gypsies are called there, bonded with the neighborhood Jews, Arabs, and poor Spaniards and took the local dances and music and layered them like they did their cast-off clothes, until they had something new—flamenco. It was the hip-hop of its time. The street art was transformed into high culture by Pushkin's legendary poem "The Gypsies" published in 1827, which in turn inspired both operas and ballets, most notably Georges Bizet's controversial *Carmen.* The opera created a scandal because it took its characters from the working class and treated their emotions with absolute seriousness. Flamenco is now one of Spain's signature cultural

Following pages: Chico and The Gipsy Kings brought their ethnic roots to the masses with Rumba Catalana, a pop-oriented version of flamenco music. The band members were born in France to Gypsy parents who had fled Spain during the Spanish Civil War.

Clockwise: Ljubica Adzovic plays a Gypsy grandmother in Emir Kusturica's *Time of the Gypsies* (1988), a film which gives insight into Gypsy life via the coming of age story of Perhan (Davor Dujmovic), a Gypsy teenager with telekinetic powers who succumbs to crime; Flamenco guitarist Manitas de Plata, November, 1966; a Gypsy dance in progress in Spain, ca. 1950; The Gipsy Kings in Camargue, in the south of France, June 2006.

exports, and *Carmen* is one of the most performed operas in history. And the character of Carmen, a promiscuous Gypsy woman, has become the most enduring Spanish style icon to date, with red roses in her loose curls, a lace tiered skirt, a cleavage-baring bodice, and a delicate pocket fan to keep the heat down.

Like the art forms they pioneered, Gypsies always managed to travel in style, especially in England, where they started to use horse-drawn caravans in the 1800s. Before that they walked, towed small carts, and slept in benders—small tents made of hazel twigs and covered in waxed canvas. Traveling showmen were the first to use caravans, but the Gypsies took the idea much further, calling their own *vardo*, after *vardon,* the Iranian word for wagon. The horse-drawn caravans were like early rock-star tour buses, built out of wood and ornamented with crazy paint jobs, pin-striping, and carved patterns lined with gold leaf. The roofs were funky and rounded, and some even had skylights. The insides looked like jewel boxes for living: They had everything one could need, including miniature kitchens, beds, and sitting areas.

The Gypsies' flamboyant style of cruising became such a source of fascination in England that it was commonly believed that their perpetual call to the road was genetic.

Today the Gypsies are still going strong. They can be found throughout Europe and Russia, with significant numbers in North and South America as well. There is little or no actual relationship between contemporary Gypsies and the Gypsetters featured in this book. However, the Gypsies' inventive nomadic history, brazen street style, and wily freelance approach to life are very much an inspiration.

A Gypsy wedding dance, 1963. Photograph by Lucien Clergue.

GYPSET TAKES OFF

Wandering with style

"You say that I am wrong for staying away too long from the center of the art world . . . The center of my art world is in my head, not anywhere else." PAUL GAUGUIN

In the 1960s Igor Cassini, a New York City gossip columnist who wrote under the pseudonym Cholly Knickerbocker, coined the term "jet set" to describe an emerging social group that was turning commercial air travel into a leisure sport. "The Jet Set is people who live fast, move fast, know the latest thing and do the unusual and the unorthodox," Cassini told *The New York Times* in 1962. "The Jet Set has no fixed rules and standards."

The jet set pioneered a new mode of living that respected neither national boundaries nor traditional pieties about thrift and sobriety. The life was, in essence, one giant, globe-trotting cocktail party that would spend a season or two at an exclusive retreat on some exotic foreign shore and then move on. Back then it was Jamaica, Sardinia, or Paradise Island in the Bahamas—retreats that were exclusive mainly because they were hard to get to. Cassini's jet set had replaced café society—the mix of daring upper-crusts, intellectuals, and beautiful (but pedigree lacking) upstarts who abandoned high society's parlors for the more democratic nightclubs and sceney restaurants of the early twentieth century. The jet set still exists today, but it has devolved into a more conventional group that slavishly follows trends and ventures to select resorts with luxury amenities, posh boutiques, and five-star restaurants. But history always seems to repeat itself, and today it's the jet set that has entered a state of decline. It's too early to tell if Gypsetters will edge out the jet set, but they certainly provide a compelling alternative. They are an influential and flourishing social group because they understand that store-bought luxury is now ubiquitous and thus boring. The lifestyles that they have built for themselves in all the corners of the world require more risk and style than cold, hard cash—which may explain why many Gypsetters are artists and adventurers.

The Gypset is new, but eccentric creatives have always been around. What follows in these chapters is a history of Gypset pioneers. It is a heritage that dates back to the nineteenth century, at least, when the poet

In the 1970s, fashion designers captured the new bohemian zeitgeist by mixing eastern and tribal wanderings with jet stream attitude. Here, a model wears flowered, gold-threaded silk pants and vest over a mousseline blouse by Mohanjeet with a fox-fur hat by Gelot. Photo by Peter Knapp for French *Elle*, 1970.

Lord Byron found that the dilapidated palazzi of the Italian Riviera were more suitable for his decadent temperament than high-society London. The adventuresses of the Victorian era, such as Jane Digby, who traded in her bulky petticoats to trek by camel around the Syrian desert with a bedouin lover, also sought refuge outside their native countries and class. In the twentieth century Ernest Hemingway showed the world that offbeat sunny spots such as Key West, Nairobi, and Havana could provide all the inspiration a writer needs. The surrealists went all out building grandiose and wacky utopias in small villages around Mexico. And Beat Generation writers Paul Bowles and William S. Burroughs created literary masterpieces out of the lawless and sun-bleached rhythms of Tangier. In the sixties and seventies an entire generation of explorers trotted the globe looking for themselves, only to come home with so much more. They set up an alternative map with anointed capitals from Goa to Ibiza to Kabul, and soon rock stars and the young fashion crowd edged in, giving the spiritual wanderings a glam lining. Which is where our tale begins.

ROAD TRIP GOES GLOBAL: THE HIPPIE TRAIL

The concept of Gypset began to emerge in earnest in the late 1960s, when the budget-minded backpacking culture collided with the moneyed jet set. Backpacking was as much a philosophical approach to life as it was a nomadic way of traveling. And nowhere was this ethos more prevalent than along the hippie trail, a loose term given to the overland route that stretched across Europe and Asia. Hordes of young hippies headed to the Continent (preferably to Amsterdam, where you could stock up on hash), bought cheap cars, and proceeded to putter south and then east along the Silk Road to the alt.anointed capitals of Istanbul, Herat, Kabul, Peshawar, Lahore, and Kathmandu. Continuing on to the balmy terrain of Southeast Asia was also popular, as a favorable exchange rate could be found in pretty much any country that practiced Eastern spirituality.

Paul Theroux chronicled the route in *The Great Railway Bazaar,* and the first guidebook, *Across Asia on the Cheap,* was published in 1973 by a young U.K. couple who had clunked across the continent in an old Austin minivan. (The book, written by Tony and Maureen Wheeler, evolved into the Lonely Planet publishing empire.) Some chose to fly: Plane tickets were not exactly cheap, but you just needed one. Once you'd arrived in an egalitarian underdeveloped country, it was possible to get by on just a few dollars. The two-week vacation was no more; these journeys of self-discovery easily extended into a few months or a few years. The whole point was to go native, crashing out in caves in Afghanistan or dancing at a Sumatran wedding, all the while wandering around in tribal sandals and robes, harem pants, chunky beads, and prayer shawls right out of Bizet's *Carmen.* The backpackers resembled the Gypsies of a hundred years earlier, but with superior luggage and walking shoes.

Throughout the 1960s and '70s Giorgio d'Sant Angelo was the go-to designer for luxe, hippie-inspired creations, such as this dress inspired by Native American adornments, Gypsy tiered skirts, and folkloric prints.

The fashion world took notice. Young designers such as Laura Jessop, Ossie Clark, and Zandra Rhodes responded with souped-up, billowing ethnic wearables and better-tailored versions of the traditional garb hanging in souks and bazaars. In Paris the haute-couture designers drew up collections that had one foot in third-world ethnic culture and the other in the jet stream. At Christian Dior, Marc Bohan upgraded the tunic with brocade and sequins. Yves Saint Laurent presented his legendary African-inspired dresses in the summer of 1967, with wooden beads, shells, and raffia that set the bar for jungle chic. Giorgio di Sant'Angelo went even further with piled-up wanderlust looks that referenced as many foreign countries as an airport departure monitor. His Scheherazade/Queen of Persia inspired getups made model Elsa Peretti look like a glamorous magic carpet, laden with heavy, embroidered brocade, her feet in tasseled rope sandals, a scarf stacked atop her head.

The six-foot-tall German model Veruschka was the poster girl of the era, turning up in body paint and tribal outfits in exotic corners from Africa to the American desert. The photographer Peter Beard took her to Kenya, where she covered herself in black shoe polish to appear like a strange and wild animal. Then she'd be in the red sands of Arizona with Italian photographer (and her lover) Franco Rubartelli, and then stylist Sant'Angelo with nothing but bolts of fabric and fur and Dynel wigs, snapping shots for *Vogue.* The fashion fantasy wasn't too far from real life. Back in the United States, the classic road trip, as defined by the boozy, carefree ideals of Jack Kerouac's *On the Road,* was getting its own makeover. After the world got a glimpse of author Ken Kesey and the Merry Pranksters, a beat-up old car and a pocketful of speed just wouldn't do. In the summer of 1964 Kesey and a group of thrill-seeking revelers decided to trek from his ranch in California to the World's Fair in New York City. For optimal kicks, the drug-addled posse resurrected an old school bus, gave it a psychedelic, Day-Glo paint job, and loaded it up with a sound system and vials of LSD. It became the gold standard for hippie caravans.

The 1969 film *Easy Rider* gave its own dirty-finger nailed props to the virtues of the open road. Two pot-smoking bikers, played by Dennis Hopper and Peter Fonda, rode free through America's back roads, partying at communes tucked into unclaimed deserts and mountains, and crashing under the stars. Even outlaw bikers, previously portrayed as dangerous and violent thugs, had been given a peaceful pass.

A decade later the bible was the new road-tripping manual *Zen and the Art of Motorcycle Maintenance* by Robert Pirsig, a metaphysical musing about the meaning of life that took place over a seventeen-day motorcycle journey across the United States. (The book was rejected by 121 publishers before it was released in 1974 and became a best seller.) Leaving town just for kicks wasn't enough anymore; the open road had become the most direct route to finding oneself. The call to wander near and far had been heard around the world. Now it was a question of where to go and what to pack.

ROCK STAR GYPSET: THE BEATLES, BOB DYLAN, AND LEONARD COHEN DROP OUT IN STYLE BUT WITHOUT ELECTRICITY

The fusion of the backpacker and the jet set became complete with the rise of the 1960s rock star. The jet set was anointing exclusive resort towns such as Gstaad, Sardinia, Saint-Tropez, and Acapulco, flitting from one to the next in Pucci dresses and toting Louis Vuitton monogrammed trunks. The rock stars could easily afford the jet-set lifestyle, but they rejected it in favor of something more soulful. They took the hippie trail and paved it over with style and glamour—the original rich hippies. Like the surrealists in the 1920s, the rock stars used travel to set up creative hives outside the mainstream. Theirs was a fur-lined leisure, but unlike the jet set, they sought out locations in India, Greece, Morocco, and Spain that were way off any high roller's map and unthinkable to those in need of running hot water, hair dryers, and tarmac runways.

The Beatles were the most famous and groovy beings on the planet in 1968. So when photos surfaced of them sitting cross-legged, wearing white tunics over striped hip-huggers, on a pink dais next to a scraggly haired, bearded yogi in the foothills of the Himalayas, it was all over. Garlands of orange flowers were draped around their waifish shoulders, and they were holding hands with some of the world's most beautiful women, including sisters Prudence and Mia Farrow—who was fresh off the set of *Rosemary's Baby* and free, following her breakup with husband Frank Sinatra. The Beatles had all the money and access in the world, but instead of luxury hotels or trendy resorts, they opted for bare feet and vegetarian food on a rustic ashram in Rishikesh, India. There couldn't have been a stronger endorsement for a glam version of the pick-up-and-go lifestyle. The Beatles were in the middle of nowhere, but looked serene as they sipped chai tea and strummed acoustic guitars with Donovan, Mike Love, and an entourage of girlfriends wrapped in colorful saris. There wasn't a more happening party anywhere in the world.

George Harrison, who had customized his Indian tunic by layering it with an embroidered vest straight from Carnaby Street, opened up to a young traveler named Paul Saltzman one afternoon between doing yoga and hanging out. "Meditation and Maharishi have helped make the inner life rich for me," said Harrison. "The meditation buzz is incredible. I get higher than I ever did with drugs. It's simple, the vibration is on the astral plane, and it's my way of connecting with God. Like, we're the Beatles after all, aren't we? We have all the money you could ever dream of. We have all the fame you could ever wish for. But it isn't love. It isn't health. It isn't peace inside. Is it?"

So what if they bolted after a couple of months when they began to suspect their guru of being a hustler? (He apparently hit on Mia Farrow and was using the Beatles to further his career.) They wrote most of their brilliant *White Album* there, and photos of the trip left an indelible mark on pop history.

Previous pages: Tunics, tasseled shawls, caftans, and other souk styles became high fashion (left). Veruschka in an exotic silk headdress embodied the era's free spirit, 1970. Photo by Franco Rubartelli (right).

Clockwise: Outlaw bikers played by Peter Fonda and Dennis Hopper inhale the new American landscape in the 1969 film *Easy Rider;* revelers at the Bardney Pop Festival outside of London in wool blankets, Gypsy layers, and a Biba bag, June 1972; The Beatles luxury hotel of choice in 1968? An Ashram in Rishikesh, India, pictured here with their wives, entourage, and the Maharishi Mahesh Yogi; Jane Birkin wearing a boho dress by Jean Bouquin, a 1960s designer with a boutique in Saint-Tropez that catered to the rich hippie set; Jimi Hendrix spent a few weeks of his short life traveling around Morocco in the summer 1969, with Cass Elliot and Michelle Phillips.

The Canadian poet and songwriter Leonard Cohen was twenty-six when he moved to the Greek isle of Hydra. It was 1960, and he had been living in a boardinghouse on the dreary streets of London. He had heard about a bohemian arts community in Hydra, so he put on his skinny black suit, bought a plane ticket, and was on his way. Cohen bought an old whitewashed building with no electricity or running water. But it had an amazing backyard terrace, which was overgrown with weeds and daisies. He set up a little table for his battered Olivetti, and with his shirt off, soaking up the sun, typed out some of his finest songs, which he performed in his now-legendary gravelly voice down the street, in a grocery store with six wooden tables. "The sun's all over my table as I write this . . . I can taste the molecules dancing in the mountains," Cohen wrote.

If a rock star showed up somewhere on the hippie trail, it was a serious endorsement. But they were selective. The town had to possess a sort of antiluxury; the high without the low looked too much like the establishment they were trying to ditch. Money might buy you a minidress and an airline ticket to a resort you'd read about in *Vogue,* but it didn't guarantee glamour once you checked in. A place was glamorous only if it had the right balance of natural beauty, interesting people, and authenticity.

Essaouira, a tiny whitewashed fishing village on the coast of Morocco, was such a place in the 1960s. Cat Stevens, Bob Marley, and Jimi Hendrix all made pilgrimages there. Hendrix arrived with his friends in a beat-up Chrysler and checked into the village's grand hotel. They wandered the wide boulevards, designed in the eighteenth century by French architect Théodore Cornut, and bargained for rugs and clothes in the souks. In the evenings Hendrix strummed a guitar around a bonfire on the beach with a collection of local musicians and itinerant hippies.

Meanwhile, a few hundred miles away, on the Mediterranean island of Ibiza, the hippies had arrived en masse and transformed the poor farming community into a boho-chic hideaway. Rock stars such as Bob Dylan, Nico, and Pink Floyd showed up as well and rented out old fincas in the pine-covered hills, composing songs and zoning out at full-moon beach parties. Dylan was said to be living in a two-hundred-year-old windmill on the nearby island of Formentera. Director Barbet Schroeder turned up to shoot his 1969 film *More*, about young heroin-addicted hippies stalled in paradise. The windmill ended up on the cover of Pink Floyd's sound track album for the film. Joni Mitchell came ashore as well and penned some of her boho masterpiece *Blue* there.

Hippies would stop on the Spanish isle for the summer, and when the weather turned, they'd fly off to the more temperate shores of Goa, India. It was the hippie-trail equivalent of the jet set's moneyed migration between its leisure enclaves of Capri in August and Acapulco in the winter. The two groups seemed to exist in parallel universes, with little contact except for the crossing of contrails. That was about to change.

"THE WHOLE POINT WAS TO GO NATIVE, CRASHING OUT IN CAVES IN AFGHANISTAN OR DANCING AT A SUMATRAN WEDDING, ALL THE WHILE WANDERING AROUND IN TRIBAL SANDALS AND ROBES, HAREM PANTS, CHUNKY BEADS, AND PRAYER SHAWLS RIGHT OUT OF BIZET'S *CARMEN*."

A master bedroom done up in luxe, worldly style with Indian fabrics on the sofa and walls and rugs from Morocco. Photo by Oberto Gili, 2006.

Opposite: Model Maggie Rizer strikes a pose in an ornate gold-lace John Galliano dress and bare feet in the City Palace of Jaipur, India. Photo by Arthur Elgort, 1999.

TRUST-FUND GYPSETTERS

Sprawled on colorful throw cushions on the roof of their nineteenth-century palace in Marrakech, Talitha and John Paul Getty, Jr., epitomized chic in the sixties. The fabulously rich and attractive young couple—he an heir to the Getty Oil fortune, she a Balinese-born Dutch fashion model—were the center of a nonstop international party. Their Palais de la Zahia was a druggy ramble of ornate rooms with inlaid ceilings, terraces patterned with glazed tiles, and hangover-shading courtyards, all hidden behind mysterious iron grilles.

When the Gettys weren't jetting between their homes in Rome and London, on shopping sprees in marketplaces in Kathmandu or on psychadelic binges in Bali and Bangkok, they threw fetes, like the "One Thousand and One Nights" party, jamming their pleasure palace with rock stars and socialites. Guests like Marie-Hélène de Rothschild lounged on mirrored pillows in one room while the Rolling Stones, Paul McCartney, and John Lennon smoked hashish in another.

"This house is really a stage," Talitha Getty, her fingers shackled in snake rings, told a reporter from *Vogue* who had been sent over with the photographer Horst to check out the scene. "Things happen here spontaneously."

The Gypsy look heads uptown in this 1968 portrait of socialite and Warhol Factory girl "Baby" Jane Holzer in a Sant'Angelo dress. *Following pages:* Talitha and J. P. Getty wearing his-and-hers caftans on the roof of their Palais de la Zahia, in Marrakech, *Vogue,* 1970.

With J. P. sporting his djellaba with Savile Row poise and Talitha in gaucho pants and an embroidered caftan, the message was clear: The days of both Palm Beach country clubs and backpacker hostels in Kabul were over. Both pastimes were hopelessly one-dimensional and boring. The Gettys, stoned and in love, had stumbled upon the perfect high-low balance; one emulated today by fashion designers such as Tom Ford and Phoebe Philo, who has dubbed Talitha's style as "couture in the souks."

Not surprisingly, Yves Saint Laurent, who kept a palace in Marrakech near the Gettys and was a fixture in their orbit, presented a North African–themed runway collection in 1970 that featured gauzy head scarves and transparent gossamer-chiffon floor-length dresses that conjured Queen Sheba by way of Rue Saint-Honoré. The next year Talitha overdosed on heroin, dying in Rome at the age of thirty-one.

Saint Laurent recalled the Gettys in 1984: "Talitha and Paul Getty lying on a starlit terrace in Marrakech, beautiful and damned, and a whole generation assembled as if for eternity where the curtain of the past seemed to lift before an extraordinary future."

Meanwhile, on the other side of the Atlantic Ocean, trust-fund Gypsetters were creating custom utopias in Mexico, building fantastic compounds that reflected a sexier,

Twiggy in a Roberto Rojas metal mesh hood, an assortment of colored Lucite rings by Bernard Kayman, and Sant'Angelo bracelets. Photo by Bert Stern, 1967.

Opposite: Gypsy dancers charm Hollywood in *The Barefoot Contessa* (1954) by Joseph L. Mankiewicz, with Ava Gardner. *This page (clockwise):* The surf film *Endless Summer,* directed by Bruce Brown in 1966, documented the new nomadic surf lifestyle with two blond surfers traveling the world in search of swell; Gina Lollobrigida in skin-baring red as the poor, barefoot Esmerelda in *The Hunchback of Notre-Dame* (1956); Romain Duris in *Gadjo Dilo* (1997), a indie film about a Parisian musician going native in a Gypsy village in Romania; Klaus Grunberg and Mimsy Farmer in *More* (1969), Barbet Schroeder's cautionary film about the casualties of the hippie trail, filmed partly on the Spanish isle of Formentera.

alternative view of the world. Artist and entrepreneur Gian Franco Brignone came of age in Italy with aesthetic utopians such as the architectural collective Superstudio, furniture designer Mario Bellini, and filmmaker Michelangelo Antonioni. Brignone constructed an experimental retreat on the Pacific coast of Mexico called Careyes for his friends, including British billionaire Jimmy Goldsmith, Italian Fiat patriarch Gianni Agnelli, and aristo-gypsetters Diane and Egon von Furstenberg. He commissioned a handful of brightly painted, surrealist, Mexican Mediterranean–style bungalows that referenced the brightly-hued modernism of Luis Barragán and the luxe rusticity of Gloria Guinness's Acapulco villa, with sprawling, palm-thatched roofs and soaring open-air rooms free of walls or windows. (One of the villas, Casa Mi Ojo, is an homage to Brignone's missing left eye, with a huge eye carved into the wall, with a pupil that doubles as a peephole, and a footbridge suspended ninety feet above the ocean that leads to a little island with meditation platforms.) It is a place where caftans and olive-branch walking sticks are prized over golf courses and yachts.

The fabulous and eccentric artist Peter Beard was a key pioneer in furthering the Gypset cause. Beard's grandfather was the tobacco heir Pierre Lorillard, who founded Tuxedo Park, New York, and is said to have invented the tuxedo. Beard grew up on Manhattan's Upper East Side and attended Yale. But instead of taking a high-yielding corporate job, he gathered up his camera and in 1955 headed to the jungles of Kenya. (He was inspired by Karen Blixon's book *Out of Africa.*) He paid for the trip with earnings from part-time work as a model and ended up buying land in the Ngong Hills, next to Blixon's coffee plantation, putting up a bunch of safari tents as his home.

The rest is history in the making: A fortieth-birthday party at Studio 54; associations with a long list of celebrated women, from Lee Radziwill to Veruschka to Iman, whom he claimed to have discovered in the African bush. "Half Tarzan, half Byron" is how Bob Colacello describes Beard in his book *Holy Terror.* Beard's lifestyle and art were all about the glamour that came with shunning convention and opting out of the traditional luxury he'd been born into. Fashion designers from Alexander McQueen to Stefano Pilati have channeled Beard for their collections. Designer Michael Kors, who cites Beard as a muse, told *The New York Times* that he has "a dangerous elegance."

"Peter is not a commercial person," his friend Iman told *Vanity Fair.* "That's his beauty and that's his downfall. He's an artist; he does not live in society; he doesn't play by their rules. He's like a wild animal. He doesn't own a pair of socks; in winter he's wearing sandals and sloshing around in the snow. He would rather have grand disasters than just have a mediocre life."

Dressed in a *kikoi,* a colorful, saronglike loincloth, Beard can still be found hobbling around barefoot—he never fully recovered from a near-death experience in which he was trampled by an elephant—on the grounds of his wild seaside acreage in Montauk, New York, which he bought in the

In the 1950s and '60s Brigitte Bardot had a penchant for disappearing into little fishing villages like Buzios and Saint-Tropez years before the crowds. Here, she easily pulls off a gone-native island look.

"TALITHA AND PAUL GETTY LYING ON A STARLIT TERRACE IN MARRAKECH, BEAUTIFUL AND DAMNED, AND A WHOLE GENERATION ASSEMBLED AS IF FOR ETERNITY WHERE THE CURTAIN OF THE PAST SEEMED TO LIFT BEFORE AN EXTRAORDINARY FUTURE." —YVES SAINT LAURENT

The designer Yves Saint Laurent lounging in his signature caftan in the garden of his Villa Oasis in Marrakech, 1980.

Opposite: Veruschka with her head and wrists wrapped in coils, wearing a silver and gold coin-shaped embroidered vest over a Turkish-style blouse. Styled by Giorgio di Sant'Angelo. Photo by Franco Rubartelli, *Vogue,* 1968.

1970s when the town was still a very remote and unfashionable corner of Long Island. There are woodsy cottages on the property where wayward Gypsetters seem welcome to lodge, few questions asked. Strewn about the feral grounds are vaguely tribal towers of piled-up stones, a zebra skull and a giraffe rib. Beard is not a surfer, but his house overlooks one of the best surf breaks. Once, during a hurricane swell, I decided to take a chance and access the water via Peter's property, uninvited. When I got to the cliff with my surfboard, there was Peter snapping photos of a model in a bikini posing on huge boulders. When he noticed me, he just took my picture and chattered on about some type of plant root. I thought that was very Gypset.

GYPSET GOES ELECTRIC: THE GLOBE TROTTING DANCE COLONY OF THE '80S AND '90S

By the mid-1980s the hippie trail had worn itself thin. Dropping out of society was no longer nearly as fashionable as working your way up to the top of it. Yuppies, corporate takeovers, and power suits would all come to define this new era. But in the hip nightclubs of London, Amsterdam, and Detroit a new electronic sound was emerging that would inspire thousands to hit the road in a remixed gypsy style. The amped-up music was best enjoyed with a few hundred people on ecstasy dancing around massive speakers cranked up all the way. So it made perfect sense for deejays and promoters to seek out venues with tolerant local officials. The old hippie enclaves of Ibiza and Goa were shoo-ins. The former hippies already had their drug connections and began to throw parties in prime forests and on beaches. They just needed a good deejay to change the sound.

The deejays came en masse, with trunks of amplifiers, mixers, computers, and power generators. Soon a transient dance colony was established, flitting between Ibiza and Goa, where heady trance parties would rage for up to four days. The deejay booths resembled religious altars, with Hindu deities, prayer rugs, and orange flowers. Between sets revelers would chill out on mats where local Indian women served chai and carrot cake for a few rupees. Soon Thailand was added to the rave map, with its full-moon parties held on the sandy beaches of Ko Pha Ngan. The party was in full swing, and more people were about to show up.

THE GYPSET AFTERPARTY: HERE'S TO THE FUTURE

At some point in the 1980s, countercultural travel began to change from off-the-beaten-path adventures into an industry—something that was increasingly commoditized. I lived in Key West for a few years as a child in the late seventies and early eighties and returned a few years later for vacation only to find that the gay culture had been wiped out by AIDS. The funky artist and hippie hangouts we used to frequent had been converted into T-shirt shops and chain hotels with restaurants with names like Olive's. The edgy boho culture and sanctuaries—like Hemingway's house—now only existed as a sanitized shout-out on the Conch Train island tour. When I went back to Paradise Island in the Bahamas, where my grandparents used to live, it had been taken over by behemoth resorts with water slides and grottos like Club Med and Atlantis.

Elsewhere the jet set and the counterculture had merged into an unappealing hybrid. Boutique hotels with chill-out cushions and scented candles now had come to represent the avant-garde. Even the off-the-grid dance circuit had turned into a cash cow: Ibiza's full-moon parties on the beach had become branded mega nightclubs. The Hamptons changed from a chic East Coast community to one big sponsored party, as did Aspen and Saint-Tropez. There were fewer and fewer places to hide. That's when the Gypset emerged.

To have an organic experience and a real social adventure, one had to be craftier and trek farther from airports and civilization, much like the hippies did in the sixties and seventies—except this time the rebellion was against excess at home, not an unpopular war in Vietnam. This could be done in small ways, like in Ibiza, for example, where Gypsetters simply moved north to the other side of the island, away from the package-tour party scene. Some pitched tepees; others renovated old, rambling whitewashed farmhouses. In the Hamptons organic thrills could still be found; you just had to look around a less obvious corner in Montauk or the Springs.

In more-extreme cases some Gypsetters joined Silicon Valley billionaires, technophiles, and thousands of other do-it-yourself types and headed to the middle of the Black Rock Desert in Nevada for Burning Man, a weeklong costume and arts happening. In January they might head off to Mali for the indigenous Tuareg music Festival Au Desert, held in Essakane, two hours from Timbuktu. A Gypset friend of mine recently told me about about a festival in Mongolia that sounded wild. (In true Gypset fashion, he intentionally left out the address.) Others might venture to Marfa, Texas, to check out the openings at Ballroom Marfa and the Judd Foundation, or to the Milwaukee International Art Fair, held twice a year in an old Polish beer hall. Of course, the really hard-core Gypsetter would never miss a full solar eclipse. See you at the next one?

Previous pages: The band Tinariwen, members of the nomadic Tuareg tribe in Mali, cofounded the Festival Au Desert, a music festival held every January in the desert outside of Timbuktu that attracts the Gypset.

DECADENT GYPSET

British romantic poets and the 24-hour palazzo party

"The farther one travels, the less one knows." LAO TZU

While the Gypset wasn't officially born until the twentieth century, a motley crew of iconic wanderers prepped their path long ago. One pioneer was Lord Byron, the British Romantic poet and an enduring muse of scandal and genius who, nearly two hundred years after his death, continues to inspire fashion designers, renaissance playboys, and hoteliers across the globe. In almost every European city of a certain run-down charm, from Rome to Sintra, Portugal, one can find dusty, wood-paneled bars and grand-dame hotels named after him.

Party hopping around London in face powder and shirts with billowing sleeves, Byron penned some of literature's most scandalous, sexually charged poems, including the satirical *Don Juan*. By 1816, at the age of twenty-eight, he had traveled the world from Albania to Spain and managed to bang out most of his best-selling epic, *Childe Harold's Pilgrimage*. He was a flagrant bisexual, had affairs with married ladies of the court, and impregnated his half sister. "Mad, bad, and dangerous to know" was what one of his lovers, Lady Caroline Lamb, wrote in her journal on the evening she first saw him. The press chronicled his every reckless move, not to mention the staggering debt that he racked up because of his penchant for fine cologne, whiskey, and cosmetics. He found Britain's mores stifling and its rules too numerous—an impossible situation for a poet. "The only virtue they honor in England is hypocrisy," he once wrote a friend.

So he packed his notebooks, inkwell, and trunks of party clothes and hopped a boat to the more tolerant shores of the Continent, where he spent the rest of his life crafting an unconventional existence. Byron's first stop was Lake Geneva, where he rented a villa next to fellow writers Percy Bysshe Shelley and his wife, author Mary Shelley, and her stepsister (with whom Byron was having

British Romantic poet Lord Byron resting in the house of a fisherman after his famous swim across the treacherous Hellespont, a narrow body of water in Turkey connecting the Aegean and the sea of Marmara.

an affair). It was in Switzerland, during a week of foggy rain and red wine, that the group composed the ghost stories that would give birth to Mary Shelley's *Frankenstein.* None of this would have been possible on the frigid streets of London.

The group, along with a revolving door of visiting writers, editors, and lovers, would spend the next decade flitting around the Continent, setting up in run-down palatial villas with cheap rents. But it wasn't total hedonism; they also managed to write some of the era's most enduring literary masterpieces, such as Percy Shelley's politically charged *Masque of Anarchy* and "To the Men of England."

A year and a half spent in a palazzo in Venice inspired Byron's most extreme creativity—and decadence. One biographer described the high times this way: "He has more lovers than most men even dream of, an enviable life style where he does not get out of bed until midday at the earliest, and a strange habit of diving into the Grand Canal for a swim—at night he carries a torch in one hand in order not to get run down by passing gondoliers. But Byron does not advertise that there is a different, professional side to his life. At midnight he sits down pen in hand to work, usually not going to bed until the light of dawn."

While in Venice, Byron famously claimed to have slept with two hundred women in as many nights, but eventually he fell in love with a young countess, whom he took, along with her family, to Pisa and Ravenna. There he became active in the insurrectionist Carbonari movement against Austrian rule.

"Lord Byron gets up at two," Shelley wrote to a friend while visiting him in Ravenna. "After breakfast we sit talking till six. From six to eight we gallop through the pine forest, which divides Ravenna from the sea; we then come home and dine, and sit up gossiping till six in the morning. I don't suppose this will kill me in a week or fortnight, but I shall not try it longer. Lord B.'s establishment consists, besides servants, of ten horses, eight enormous dogs, three monkeys, five cats, an eagle, a crow, and a falcon; and all these, except the horses, walk about the house . . ."

The group moved on to the sunny and idyllic fishing villages on the Gulf of La Spezia, on the Italian Riviera, where they all rented villas and briefly published *The Liberal,* a radical political journal. (In England journalists and writers who expressed dissenting political views could be charged with treason and imprisoned.) Unfortunately, the whole party came to an end when Shelley's schooner sank in a storm and he drowned while crossing the bay. Soon after, Byron headed to Greece, having impetuously decided to join the war against the Ottomans, despite being hopelessly overweight. He had a heart attack in a boat on the way to battle, a poetic ending at sea in 1824.

An engraving of Lord Byron in his study. *Following pages:* Sir Richard Francis Burton (1821–1890) traveled extensively in Africa and Asia, and managed to sneak into Mecca, disguised as an Afghan pilgrim. He spoke more than 25 languages and led a controversial sex life (left). Lady Jane Digby traded life in England for one of worldly adventure, living in Corfu, Athens, and Albania before marrying a Bedouin tribesman in Syria. Portrait by Carl Haag, 1862. Taraq Rajab Museum, Kuwait (right).

ECCENTRIC VICTORIAN ADVENTURESSES AND EXPLORERS: DJELLABAS AND PETTICOATS ON THE CAMEL ROUTE

There are two basic types of explorers. The high-octane challenger who wears Patagonia, munches PowerBars, and desperately wants to trek up difficult mountain peaks, heli-ski in virgin snow, or paddle through the Arctic in a carbon-fiber kayak to eat blubber burgers with Eskimo. Then there is what I call the alternative explorer, or alt.explorer, who is more comfortable chilling under a goatskin tent in the Sahara with the Tuareg for a few years, dressing in sarongs, or surfing off the coast of Micronesia for the season.

The distinction was never clearer than in Victorian England. From the 1830s to the early 1900s the British Empire controlled nearly one-quarter of the world's population (thus the popular saying "The sun never sets on the British empire"). For a Brit it was possible, at least conceptually, to set up anywhere—India, Africa, even Australia. But just as these "exotic" cultures were being volleyed into the mainstream imagination by adventure writers such as Joseph Conrad and explorers like Richard Burton, Victorian England was easily the most restrictive and oppressive society in Western civilization, especially if you were a woman.

Women had few rights and were basically the property of their husbands. They were not allowed to divorce unless cruelty or adultery was involved—although, for a man, his wife's infidelity was sufficient grounds. If a woman felt like taking a swim, she was expected to arrive at the water's edge in a bathing machine: A small, shedlike structure on big wagon wheels that was pulled into the sea so women could dive in without being glimpsed in their giant bathing costumes. Needless to say, surfing or boogie boarding would have been out of the question.

Jane Digby, a beautiful aristocrat, was all but chased out of London at the age of twenty-two. She had already been married off to a much older baron, become pregnant by an Austrian prince, and had just weathered a front-page divorce trial. Digby traveled to Switzerland answering her true calling as an alt.adventuress. She inspired future generations of women as well as eight novels that featured mainly scandalous portrayals, including one by Honoré de Balzac. She was fluent in nine languages and lived for spells in France, Germany, Corfu, and Athens, fully integrating herself into each destination by shacking up with a string of local kings, princes, barons, counts, and most notably, a dragoman—a sort of traveling diplomat—from Jaffa. For a time she was the lover of a cave-dwelling Albanian general, riding Arabian horses at breakneck speed, and hunting game for food on the steep mountain trails.

But her star turn came when Digby was in her forties and headed to Syria to attempt the dangerous trek to Palmyra, an oasis in the middle of the desert. When most women were stuffed

Isabelle Eberhardt (1877–1904) grew up in Switzerland but spent her adult life wandering around North Africa in drag atop a camel, ca. 1900.

into petticoats, Digby was galloping through the desert on what she later called "the greatest adventure, probably, of all my journeys."

According to a story in *The New York Times:*

> "She wore an *aba,* or cloak, over a djellaba, and a square white kaffiyeh . . . . On her feet, she wore lemon yellow kid ankle boots with pointed toes. Her guide, Medjuel el Mezrab, a Bedouin sheik, wore what he usually wore, which is to say, a scarlet cloak over a striped djellaba, a bright silk kaffiyeh and red leather boots with upturned toes. He had tied several silk scarves in a wide sash around his waist, which served as a holster for his knives and pistols, and around his neck hung a sword on a silk cord. He wore his final accessory, a hooded hawk, on his wrist."

Of course, Digby fell in love with the handsome bedouin guide, twenty years her junior. They married, much to the horror of London society, and Digby lived the rest of her life in high renegade style, spending half the year in an opulent palace she had built in Damascus, where she hosted parties for the likes of Richard Burton, who had become the consul to Damascus, and his wife, Isabel. The other half of the year she traveled with the Mezrab tribe in the desert, living a nomadic existence in the black goat-hair tents of Arabia.

The writer Isabelle Eberhardt was another alt.explorer cut from the same caftan. The daughter of a British aristocrat and a Russian émigré, the androgynous-looking Eberhardt decided at the age of twenty to pack in her boring and restricted life in Switzerland and head to North Africa. But instead of relying on chaperones and servants, as was the custom for a young unmarried woman in 1890s, Eberhardt decided it would be much easier to pull back her hair, toss on a djellaba, and cruise around on a camel, dressed as a man. She even came up with an alter ego: Si Mahmoud Essadi. In full drag, she island hopped around the Mediterranean, landing in Sardinia decades before the jet set would lay claim to it. But her main stomping grounds were the deserts of Algeria and Tunisia, where for years she slept under the stars in yurts and banded with the locals to fight French colonial rule. She converted to the austere Wahhabi form of Islam but still partied like a rock star, knocking back prodigious amounts of alcohol, chain-smoking hashish, and sleeping with whomever she pleased.

An eyewitness from that time said of her: "She was an alcoholic [but] deeply religious . . . She was passionate, sensual, but not in a woman's way. And she was completely flat-chested . . .

When she saw a man she wanted, she took him. She'd beckon him over, and off they'd go . . . And whatever she did, she remained well-bred."

Eberhardt wrote articles for French newspapers and kept a journal that Paul Bowles later transcribed into a book called *The Oblivion Seekers.*

"Right now I long for only one thing," Eberhardt wrote in her journal from the isles of the Mediterranean. "To reclothe myself in that cherished personality, the real and true one, and to go back to Africa again. I long to sleep in some sort of chaotic camp surrounded by friends made on the spot among Spahis and nomads."

Back on the Continent, stockbroker-turned-Impressionist-painter Paul Gauguin felt the pull, too. In the 1880s many freethinkers and penniless intellectuals abandoned Europe. The far-flung colonial outposts, just a boat ride away, provided the ultimate dream escape. Like his friend Vincent van Gogh, with whom he spent a few months painting in the French town of Arles, Gauguin experienced bouts of depression and at one time attempted suicide. He was disillusioned with Impressionism and felt that it had become formulaic and superficial. By contrast, the art of Africa and Asia seemed far more mystic and meaningful. Gauguin had made several attempts to find a tropical paradise where he could "live on fish and fruit" and paint in his increasingly primitive style.

In 1887 he went to Panama to work on the canal project, but was fired after two weeks. Then he stopped briefly at the Caribbean isle of Martinique. He was intensely inspired by the tropics and their vibrant colors and primitive, innocent-seeming cultures. The very next year Gauguin abandoned his tried-and-true style of European Impressionism and began honing his signature bold fantasy colors and large sunny shapes. Van Gogh and Gauguin plotted their new lives in exotic lands where money and prosecution would not be daily pressures. Van Gogh was too depressed to make it (this was about when he chopped off his ear), but Gauguin, after spending an afternoon in the 1890s at the Universal Exposition in Paris at a pavilion dedicated to the South Pacific in the 1890s, decided to make the journey to the soft shores of Tahiti. He sold thirty paintings to Edgar Degas, set sail, and never really looked back. He spent the rest of his life living in a little grass hut, surrounded by beautiful, naked women and producing his most famous paintings.

Following pages: Paul Gauguin, *Woman Holding a Fruit*, oil on canvas, 1893 (left). His 14-year-old model, Vahine Vaeoho Marie Rose, wearing missionary finery in the village of Atuona in the Marquesas (right).

P Gauguin 93
haere ia oe

MACHO GYPSET: ERNEST HEMINGWAY EASILY STUMBLES INTO THE WORLD'S COOLEST CORNERS

Thirty years and a world war later, it was the Americans who embodied the spirit of the latent Gypset. And nobody blazed the trail harder than the writer Ernest Hemingway, who had a knack for getting to the coolest corners of the world way before everyone else. "You ought to see the Spanish Coast," Hemingway wrote to Sherwood Anderson in 1921 while sailing to Galicia. "Big brown mountains looking like tired dinosaurs."

Most of the expat writers of the Lost Generation of the 1920s congregated in Paris, because America was seen as too provincial and close-minded—and because the cost of living was lower in postwar Europe. Intellectuals like Anderson, F. Scott Fitzgerald, Ezra Pound, Waldo Peirce, T. S. Eliot, and Gertrude Stein could loll away the hours in cozy Montparnasse cafés and lead romantic existences in Parisian town houses. But Paris was just a temporary stopover for Hemingway. By the age of twenty-five, he had seen Italy, Spain, Germany, Switzerland, Austria, and Constantinople. Over the course of his life he would travel to places as far-flung as Africa, Cuba, Hong Kong, Hawaii, and London.

I'll never forget driving down a bumpy dirt road in Cabo Blanco, in the remote north of Peru, to a tiny fishing village. My guide pointed to an old, beached fishing boat and said it was Hemingway's. We went into a dusty bar tucked among the rocks, and the ancient bartender showed me a sun-faded photo on the wall of him serving Hemingway a beer in the 1950s. It confirmed what I already knew: Hemingway had been to almost every out-of-the-way paradise that I'd been to or wanted to go to.

In true Gypsetter fashion, he didn't so much travel as wander until he discovered an offbeat place that particularly inspired him. Then he would find some ramshackle, once-grand house and set up for a couple of years to write. Hemingway didn't try to blend in like the Victorian explorers; he would never dress in anything as experimental or spiritual as a fez or a caftan. Instead, he would show up on the narrow cobblestone streets of a small town in khakis, a loose-fitting white button-down shirt rolled up to his elbows, carrying an old typewriter. (In Cuba, though, he was occasionally spotted wearing a guayabera shirt.) The other criteria for choosing his locales were some sort of macho blood sport, like hunting or fishing, and a dark local bar with a particular seamy charm (Harry's Bar in Venice; Café Iruña in Pamplona, Spain; Sloppy Joe's in Key West). The best-selling author, who won a Pulitzer for *The Old Man and the Sea,* was completely uninterested in mainstream life and preferred to chronicle the characters and outsiders.

While in Paris, Hemingway, who was still struggling to start his career, took a suggestion from Gertrude Stein and settled for a while in Pamplona. There he befriended matadors and

Author Ernest Hemingway at his home in Havana with a group of his beloved cats feeding at his feet, ca. 1940s.

famously documented the festival of San Fermín's running of the bulls, the inspiration for his novel *The Sun Also Rises.*

When the Great Depression hit, most of his fellow expats in Paris had run their bank accounts dry; they returned to the United States to find jobs in New York and other cities. Hemingway, however, was just getting started with his alternative way of life. His friend and fellow novelist John Dos Passos suggested he move to the remote and somewhat lawless isle of Key West. (Prohibition was still in effect, but Key West was so far away that the usual rules did not apply.) Hemingway lured his new wife, Pauline (number two of four), to Key West with the promise that a new car would be waiting for her. Unfortunately, there were no roads or cars on the island. When persuading his friends to come visit, Hemingway proudly dubbed the Florida Keys "the Saint-Tropez of the poor."

Hemingway's entourage began to arrive in droves on the rickety railroad from Miami. The small island had been officially anointed by the intelligentsia. Hemingway held court in his stately Spanish-style conch house, built of heavy limestone and set amid bougainvillea, palm trees, and hundreds of cats. Pauline's wealthy uncle had given them the house as a wedding present. (A Gypsetter might live in a mud hut or a dilapidated mansion, but never in a quaint dwelling. And if it is a mansion, it has usually been obtained through some amount of cunning—say, a loan from a wealthy relative or friend—or else in such a state of grand disrepair that it has been overlooked.)

During this period, Hemingway took frequent fishing trips to Havana and went hunting in Kenya. He was inspired by *Out of Africa,* a memoir by the controversial Danish baroness Karen von Blixen-Finecke, who wrote under the pseudonym Isak Dinesen. She had moved to the colonial Ngong Hills near Nairobi to start a coffee plantation with her husband in 1914. They separated a few years later, and she managed the farm by herself for a decade. (Blixen was also a muse for artist and Gypset forefather Peter Beard, whose Hog Ranch is just down the road from her former property.)

By the late 1930s Hemingway was a famous war correspondent and author. After Key West and a divorce, he decided to move even further out of the mainstream and set up in Havana, which at the time was an inexpensive but beautiful no-rules party town for America's wealthy. There was also cockfighting and amazing marlin fishing—the perfect place for Hemingway. He and wife number three, Martha Gellhorn, found a run-down fifteen-acre estate just outside of downtown Havana called Finca Vigía (Lookout Farm). Hemingway decorated the home where he penned *Islands in the Stream, The Old Man and the Sea,* and a *Moveable Feast* in his signature style: floor to ceiling piles of books and horned hunting trophies mounted in almost every room. To Hemingway, Cuba, with its seedy, offbeat charm, was pure literature in motion.

Finca Vigía, Hemingway's hillside estate outside of Havana, where he lived from 1939 until 1960. The airy rooms were filled with mounted stag heads, books, and bottles of rum.

SURREALISTS IN MEXICO: THE REVOLUTION IN HUARACHE SANDALS AND PEASANT BLOUSES

André Breton founded surrealism, a literary and art movement inspired by Freudianism, in Paris in 1924. Breton authored the Surrealist Manifesto, which promoted the expression of imagination revealed in dreams. His statement, which was expanded upon by legions of writers and artists, from Salvador Dalí to René Magritte, was an ultraleftist attack on rational society. The surrealists did everything they could to promote Karl Marx's idea of communism and annoy the establishment.

It was an international group, hailing from Spain to South America, and they traveled en masse wherever they were invited. Often the invitations came from wealthy patrons who allowed them to remake their country houses as temporary utopias, with costumes and absurdist dinner parties. In the summer of 1939, the surrealists famously rented a French château at Chemilleu, where a group including Spanish painter Esteban Francés, Chilean artist Roberto Matta, American painter Kay Sage, and Breton sprawled on the lawns painting, exchanging ideas, and reciting poetry.

But it was the eve of the Second World War, and many of the surrealists thought it safer to leave the Continent than live on European soil. Moving to Mexico, a surreal spot in itself, seemed like the best exit strategy; a heady international surrealist-in-exile scene was in full swing there. Diego Rivera and Frida Kahlo, draped in her folkloric drag, were at the peak of their fame, holding court in Mexico City at Kahlo's Casa Azul, where monkeys swung from trees and peacocks preened in the electric blue courtyard. Better still, Leon Trotsky, the exiled Bolshevik and Marxist theorist, and his wife were also living with Kahlo. Trotsky, a political Gypsetter of sorts, had been wandering the planet ever since his archrival Stalin had tossed him out of Russia after the Communist revolution. Trotsky lived for a while on an island off the coast of Istanbul, and near Oslo, Norway. He ended up in Mexico after Kahlo urged President Lázaro Cárdenas to grant him asylum. Trotsky was a rare and strange trophy for the surrealists and ignited a full-scale migration to Mexico; the group included Breton, Wolfgang Paalen, Remedios Varo, and Esteban Francés.

The exiles' party only got better when wealthy English painter Gordon Onslow Ford showed up with his American wife, Jacqueline Johnson, a nature conservationist. The couple, who had been part of Breton's surrealist crew in Paris, wanted to set up a country hideaway. They discovered a remote village called Erongarícuaro in the hills of Michoacán. To get to the small town, populated by Tarascan Indians, one had to putter for hours on lumpy mountain roads and then hop a boat across Lake Pátzcuaro. There Onslow Ford and Johnson played host in a large abandoned mill that they named El Molino. The industrial space was transformed into living and studio spaces. For the next six years, El Molino became a secret utopia for the surrealists. They adopted a boho

French poet Rene Char with writer and artist André Breton in Marseilles, 1941.
Following pages: Surrealist painter Salvador Dalí in a fisherman's cottage in Port Lligat, Spain, 1957 (left).
Mexican artist Frida Kahlo was a catalyst for the surrealist movement in Mexico, ca. 1950 (right).

look, kicking around the village in huarache sandals and peasant blouses and joining in the native Indian ceremonies. Johnson helped Wolfgang Paalen with his journal DYN, and some claim that it was in Erongarícuaro that Breton and Trotsky wrote the famed manifesto *Pour un art révolutionnaire indépendent* (published under the names of Breton and Diego Rivera), which called for "complete freedom of art."

Meanwhile, a few hundred miles north of Mexico City, in the town of Xilitla in the Sierra Gorda mountains, the wealthy English art patron Sir Edward James was slumming it in the jungle, constructing his own "surrealist Xanadu" on an old coffee plantation.

An early trust-fund Gypsetter, Sir Edward was heir to a copper and timber fortune and the godson of King Edward VII. There were also rumors that he was the king's illeigitamate son. He was a major patron of the surrealists and hung out with Dalí, Magritte, and Dylan Thomas in Europe. "Edward is crazier than all the surrealists put together," his friend Piccaso once gossiped to Sigmund Freud. "They pretend, but he is the real thing." He made the Hollywood scene in the 1940s, befriending Man Ray and Aldous Huxley; the latter turned him on to the Vedanta movement, where he met all sorts of early New Agers.

In Cuernavaca, Mexico, Sir Edward met a charismatic manager of a local telegraph office who helped him find his surrealist paradise, where he could express his bizarre dreams through wild gardens of exotic plants and animals. He named his land Las Pozas, in a dense tropical forest with wild parrots, mangoes, bamboo, and oversized ferns, and set out to construct his vision: Eighty acres of towering concrete sculptures with names like the Temple of the Ducks and the House Destined to Be a Cinema. A pair of giant concrete hands stick out of the ground and a staircase winds high up into the clouds. Sir Edward had once said that he "wanted a Garden of Eden set up . . . and I saw that Mexico was far more romantic." To each his own garden.

A stone orchid in Las Pozas, a surrealist sculpture garden built in the jungle of Xilitla, Mexico, by British aristocrat Sir Edward James in the 1950s and '60s.

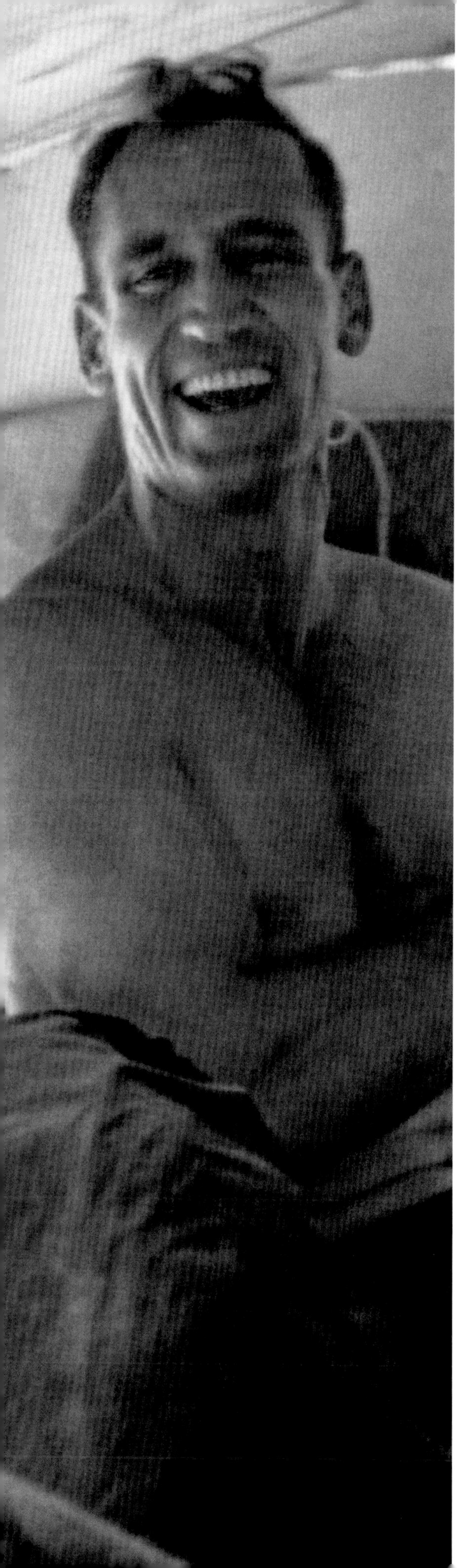

TRANSIENT CHIC: ON THE ROAD WITH MIDCENTURY BEATNIKS, SURFERS, AND BIKER GANGS

> "It was drizzling and mysterious at the beginning of our journey. I could see that it was all going to be one big saga of the mist. 'Whooee!' yelled Dean. 'Here we go!' And he hunched over the wheel and gunned her; he was back in his element, everybody could see that. We were all delighted, we all realized we were leaving confusion and nonsense behind and performing our one and noble function of our time, move."
>
> —Jack Kerouac, *On the Road* (1957)

After the Second World War the seeds of America's first pop counterculture were pushing through the gloss. Throngs of young men returned from the war and faced bummer jobs, mortgage payments on poorly designed tract homes, and insidious kitchen appliances. And in this stifling blueprint, women were cast as neatly coiffed wardens. Those who couldn't deal turned to pills and booze. Not surprisingly, the best-selling novel of the era was Sloan Wilson's dark *Man in the Gray Flannel Suit.*

Not everyone played along. Factions of this postwar generation, rebels without a cause who were unable to come down from

After a cross-country trek on LSD and amphetamines, The Merry Pranksters' Further bus driver Neal Cassady meets Dr. Timothy Leary (foreground) at his farm in Millbrook, New York, 1964.

the thrill of being posted in faraway lands, set out to create alternative lifestyles that were subversively nomadic and flagrantly anticommercial.

Some took on surfing as a way of life. They flocked to the shores of Hawaii and Southern California and idled away the days amid the lineup of beautiful, tanned physiques as America glanced disapprovingly from commuter traffic jams. The surfers made being broke look cool and defiant and inspired the buff dropouts in the surfploitation films that appeared a decade later. They surfed all day, ate abalone from the sea, and then slept on the beach in groovy grass huts. And they kept on doing it well after the summer sun had faded.

John Grissim, in his book *Pure Stoke*, explained it this way: "What fueled [their] great passion, was their new independence, and an unwillingness to drop back into a regimented social system. The stance was not angry, it was go-it-alone, laissez-faire, unconsciously romantic, and a bit escapist. But that life was based on a clear, clean, passionate vision that was attainable—as were the waves. Whenever and wherever the swell was up, there was always plenty of room."

Surfers like Mike Doyle and Pat Curren traveled the world by any means possible, colonizing sleepy coastal towns that have since become shrines on the Gypset map, such as the North Shore of Oahu, Lima, Malibu, and Australia's Byron Bay. Hollywood took notice and Technicolored their dropout ethos with films like *Surf Crazy* and *Ride the Wild Surf*, not to mention chart-topping tunes by the Beach Boys and Jan and Dean. The 1966 surf safari movie *The Endless Summer,* about two young blond surfers scoping the globe, from South Africa to Indonesia, in propeller planes and crowded buses, made it clear that surfers were the ultimate cool nomads.

Meanwhile, another rogue group of postwar veterans decided to escape normalcy via motorcycle. In the mid-1940s they began to form daredevil gangs such as the Booze Fighters, the Pissed Off Bastards, and the Diablos. The gangs were hardly the drug-running, violent speed freaks that they would become in the sixties and seventies. They were young and restless men, fresh from a war, with an above-average knowledge of mechanics. Motorcycles, sold as army surplus, were the cheapest, loudest, and most visceral way out of the cul-de-sac. Riding them was pure wind-beating freedom. The gangs lived communally in clubhouses or at vagabond campsites and flaunted greasy hair, tattoos, and lots of leather to promote a menacing freedom. But soon motorcycle gangs got out of control. Marlon Brando's 1953 film *The Wild One* was based on the true, if exaggerated, story of a menacing bandit gang of bikers commandeering a small California town in 1947.

The bikers' more intellectual peers, the beatniks, staged their own rebellion in the cafés and bookshops of Greenwich Village and San Francisco's North Beach. Instead of using their brilliant minds and Ivy

Jack Kerouac (1922–1969) types a poem in the New York City apartment of photographer Fred McDarrah in 1959 based on his road trip from San Francisco to New York with Albert Saijo and Lew Welch. A condensed version was later published as "Trip Trap."

ON THE ROAD

Reverting to a Simpler style —

Further draft & beginnings — Nov. 1949

ITINERARY & PLAN

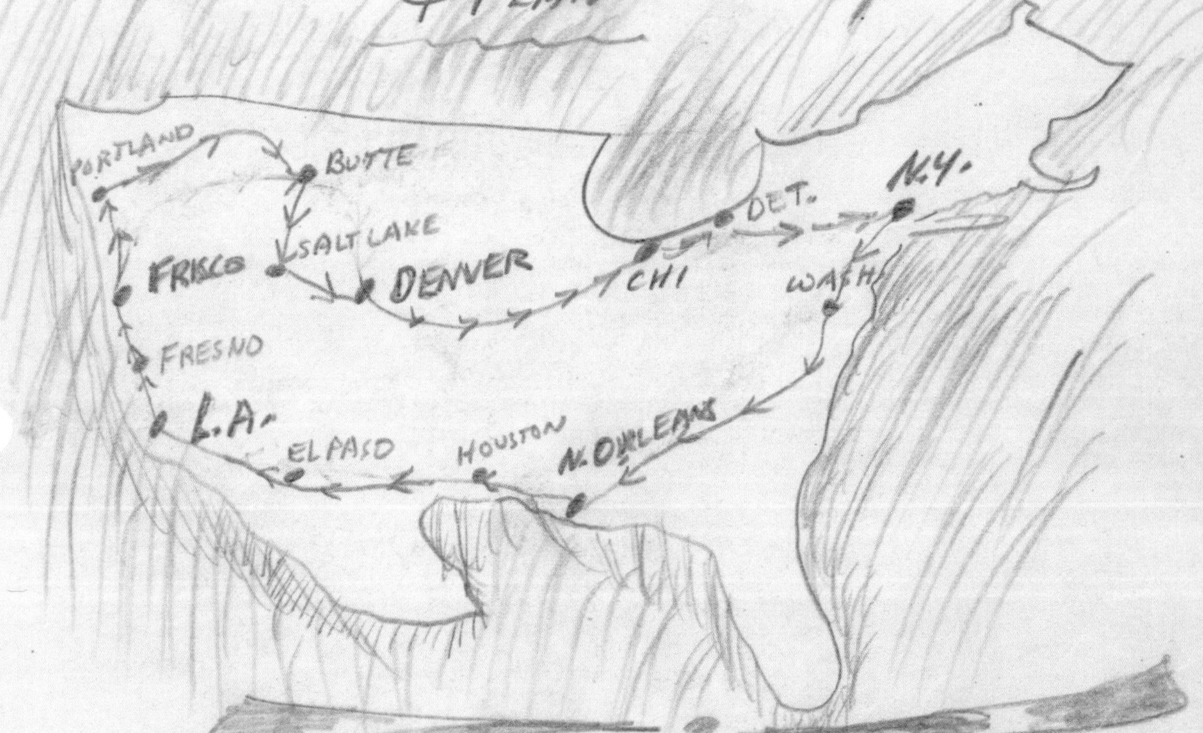

1. New York Jail
2. Times Square I
3. Road to New O'leans
4. New Orleans
5. Road to Frisco
6. Frisco (+ Valley)
7. Road to Butte
8. Butte
9. Road to Denver
10. Denver
11. Road to New York
12. Times Square Again

From May to May

CHARACTERS

Red Moultrie
Clem Lemke
Slim Jackson
Old Bull
Dean Pomeray
Marylou
Evelyn Johnson

Mrs. Moultrie
Elena
Old Moultrie
Laura Moultrie
Laurette.
And Various Shades

Opposite: A page from a notebook Kerouac used in writing *On the Road*. Courtesy of The New York Public Library. *This page (from top)*: Writer Paul Bowles in his trademark ex-pat gentlemens attire in Morocco, 1956; Beatnik author William S. Burroughs stops at a sidewalk cafe in the Petit Socco during a trip to Tangier; Tangier was a lawless paradise for artists and eccentrics in the 1940s and '50s; singer-songwriter Leonard Cohen liked to steal away to the small Greek island of Hydra in the Saronic Gulf to write and compose; an artists' retreat on a Greek island, 1960; Allen Ginsberg relaxing in a no-frills boarding house, Tangier, July 1961.

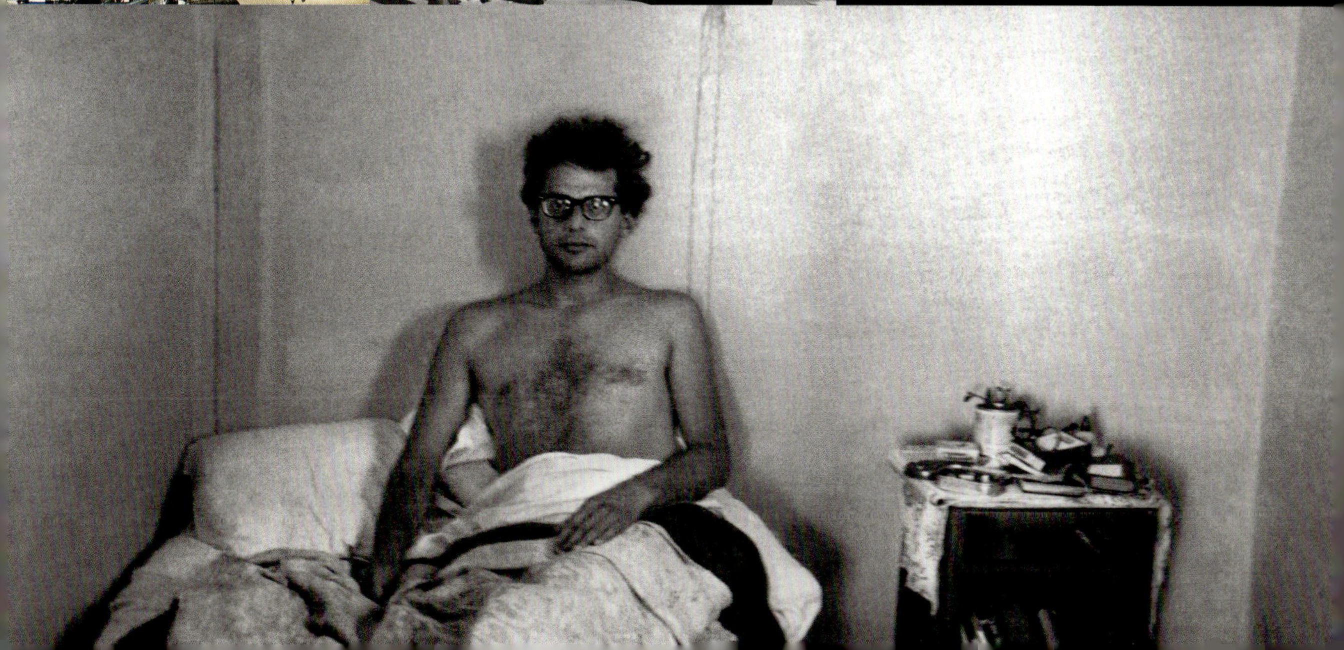

League educations to earn white-collar salaries, they rejected the corporate structure and found artistic expression on the road with hobos and other marginal transients.

Leading the charge was Jack Kerouac—the son of immigrants, from the poor factory town of Lowell, Massachusetts—whose novel *On the Road* inspired a generation to leave it all behind. Kerouac wrote the book in three weeks in 1951, on a long roll of tracing paper he taped together so he wouldn't have to waste time changing pages. When *On the Road* came out six years later after being rejected by several publishers, *The New York Times* declared Kerouac the voice of a generation.

Along with Kerouac's friends Neal Cassady, William S. Burroughs, and Allen Ginsberg, the beats extolled a lifestyle in which all that was needed were a few dollars, a full tank of gas, and, with any luck, a pocket full of Benzedrine. Suddenly, college kids across America were forgoing their country club memberships for rucksacks and rugged blue jeans. Not only was the open road freedom, it was also free. Who needed pricey airplane tickets and expensive hotel rooms when you could hitch a ride in a battered old Chevy and crash on a friend's couch along the way? It was pretty obvious from *On the Road* and the photos of travel-addicted youth plastered across *Life* magazine who was having more fun.

LAWLESS TANGIER: THE BEATS DISCOVER THE HEADY MAGIC OF SOUKS, KIF, AND YOUNG MOROCCAN BOYS

In the late 1940s a Gypset enclave was building on the winding, rule-free streets of Tangier, Morocco. The city was an international zone, governed by a commission of nations; for all practical purposes, this meant the city was not being governed at all. Pretty much anything was tolerated besides rape and murder. Homosexuality was the norm, drugs were abundant, and eccentricity was rewarded. Needless to say, outcast internationals arrived by the boatload.

New York literary darlings Paul and Jane Bowles found themselves in the middle of the city's decadent social circles with European aristocrats and other fellow expats, such as Woolworth heiress Barbara Hutton and artist Brion Gysin, who set up in old palaces on Old Mountain. Hutton was renowned in Gypset circles and throughout Europe for the over-the-top soirees that she hosted in her stone palace in the casbah. At these decadent gatherings one could find the likes of Charlie Chaplin and Aristotle Onassis wandering among hired belly dancers, camel drivers, and nomadic tribesmen with skin stained blue from the dye of their robes. Coincidentally, it was Gertrude Stein who in the 1930s gave Bowles, whom she had met in Paris, the idea to go to Tangier, just as she had advised Hemingway to go to Pamplona, Spain. With its costume parties in old *riads* and medina palaces, Tangier soon became the port of call for slumming literati like Truman Capote, Tennessee Williams, and Cecil Beaton, as well as thousands of wannabes.

"Before coming here you should do three things," Capote famously wrote in 1950. "Be inoculated for typhoid, withdraw your savings from your bank, say goodbye to your friends—heaven knows you may never see them again . . . Because Tangier is a basin that holds you."

For Paul Bowles, Tangier provided the escape he had always searched for. He had been a music columnist for the *New York Herald Tribune* but was beginning to stagnate in the city. So in 1947, at the age of 37, he and Jane set sail for Tangier. He penned *The Sheltering Sky* while traveling through the Sahara, holed up in basic hostels, typing out the words as he lay in bed in silk pajamas.

Michelle Green, in her book *The Dream at the End of the World,* describes the classic Gypset way in which Bowles traveled.

"He took with him vast amounts of luggage—most of which contained a wardrobe more suitable for a sojourn in London than an excursion in rural Spain and North Africa. Tweed jackets, silk ties, and dressing gowns, oxford cloth shirts, cashmere vests and pullovers—with the exception of the djellaba he occasionally affected, the decorous Paul declared himself to be at a distinct remove from his surroundings."

Beat writer William S. Burroughs showed up in Tangier in 1953 mostly as a last resort. There were few places the deviant morphine addict could go to escape his looming legal problems in the United States (where he faced numerous drug charges) and Mexico (where he had shot and killed his common-law wife during a drunken game). The skinny Harvard graduate had always been enamored of Bowles's fiction, so he came to Tangier, arriving by boat, wearing his trademark black Greenwich Village threads and dark gray hat, a very impractical attempt to shade his cadaverous complexion from the searing Mediterranean sun. He rented a single room with a garden in a male brothel called Villa Muneria and famously wrote *Naked Lunch* while stoned out of his mind.

Soon enough, his roaming beatnik brethren arrived, including Gregory Corso, Allen Ginsberg, and Jack Kerouac. They spent their days smoking kif, editing, typing, and experimenting with Brion Gysin and Burroughs's new cut-up technique. Nights were spent smoking more kif, hooking up with young Moroccan boys, and carousing at Gysin's restaurant, the 1001 Nights, whose house band hailed from the village of Joujouka. It was a more decadent version of Rick's Café Américain. Nothing was off-limits; all experiments with life and art were fair game. For a moment in time, Tangier was an idyllic creative refuge, a template for Gypset capitals in the years to come.

THE GYPSETTERS

Contemporary far-out lifestyles

The Gypset map looks a lot different than your average atlas; instead of New York, London, or Moscow its capitals stretch from Ibiza, Montauk, to Padang Padang. Many Gypsetters just flit about from one place to the next and camp out on daybeds, in guest rooms, tepees, and yurts with friends. While others, like the artists, musicians, surfers, and bon vivants featured in this chapter, have constructed personal utopias that reimagine a groovier retreat.

In the pages that follow are several Gypsetters who I have met—or wanted to meet—in my travels over the last few years. Each has seamlessly created the perfect dream perch for a nomadic and experimental lifestyle. And each has handpicked a location for their set up that is still somewhat undiscovered with that special secret allure.

There is the French adventuress Carolyn Roumeguere who commutes between a tree house in the Kenyan section of the Rift Valley and an old cottage on the jungley island of Manda near Lamu; Marni designer Consuelo Castiglioni who keeps a Bedouin tent on the Balearic island of Formentera atop a rocky cliff that she sprinkled with silver pebbles and purple marbles; the artist Andrea Zittel with her desert compound in Joshua Tree, California, where guests shouldn't be alarmed to find themselves snoozing in the yard amongst creosote and cactus in metal capsule-like sleeping pods that she calls Wagon Stations.

And there are more Gypsetters; an Argentine hotelier with a psychedelic beach sprawl in Uruguay, an art star with a houseboat on the Thames; a pair of French bon vivants with a chic matrilineal surf lair overlooking the best break in Sayulita, Mexico; a British fashion designer who holds court in tepees amongst the tall grass of her families farm in Somerset, and more.

Life on the island of Lamu, Kenya: windswept dunes protect the fort. Photo by Sasha Eisenman.

JADE JAGGER

Jade Jagger may well be the ultimate Gypset offspring. She was hanging out in Saint-Tropez when it was still cool, back in 1971—albeit in her mother's womb. Nicaraguan-born Bianca Perez Morena de Macias was four months pregnant and wearing a white Yves Saint Laurent pantsuit when she said "I do" to Jade's father, Mick Jagger of the Rolling Stones. The vows were exchanged at the Saint-Tropez town hall and cheered on by barefoot hippies and besuited socialites alike. They came on bicycles and in Rolls-Royce limousines—and sometimes it was the barefoot hippies who stepped out of the limousines.

Before the wedding the Jaggers shacked up nearby in Keith Richards's rented Villa

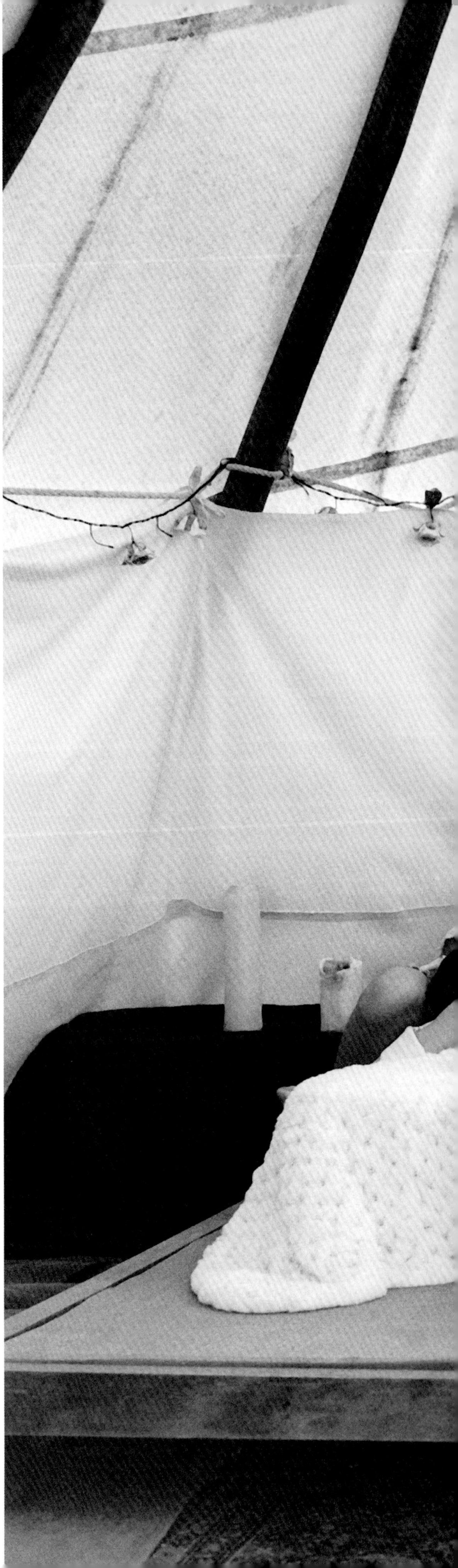

Nellcôte, a sixteen-room mansion on the waterfront in Villefranche, between Nice and Monaco. There the band spent a few months recording *Exile on Main Street*—and throwing the ultimate house party. So it was not surprising that for two days after the baby was born, she went unnamed. Mick and Bianca decided on the name Jade because, as Mick told a reporter, "She is very precious and quite, quite perfect."

Jagger's part-time babysitter in New York City, Andy Warhol, let her frolic among the props and fabulous people at the Factory. "I love Mick and Bianca, but Jade's more my speed," Warhol famously gushed. "I taught her how to color, and she taught me how to play Monopoly. She was four, and I was forty-four. Mick was jealous. He said I was a bad influence because I gave her champagne."

These days Jagger has her own jewelry and fashion lines based in London. (She also has a lucrative side job designing interiors for a luxury-condo development group in Manhattan.) When not working, she's roaming the Gypset map, jetting to the shores of Goa, India; the Caribbean island of Mustique, which she remembers from the pre-trendy days of her childhood, when there was one telephone line and one generator for the whole place; and Cornwall, a chilled-out surfing community on a tip of rugged coastline in southwest England.

But Ibiza, with its languid sunlight and permanent population of well-traveled eccentrics, feels most like home to her. When Jagger first discovered Ibiza, in 1996, the Spanish isle had been dismissed by the glamorous set as a hippie backwater, overtaken by hordes of ecstasy-addled ravers from Brighton, who piled into package-tour high-rises. But Jagger recognized the island's undercurrent of bohemian allure, and soon the fashion flock did, too. Phoebe Philo, Jean-Paul Gaultier, and Mario Testino have all been spotted on the winding streets of Eivissa, checking out the vintage wares at Ganesha, or sunning up-island at clothing-optional beaches such as Aguas Blancas or Benirras. These are beaches where on Sundays there are still drum circles at sunset. If the island's hidden corners look familiar now, it is because of Missoni, Gucci, Louis Vuitton, and Roberto Cavalli. Photographers like Mert Alas and Marcus Piggott, who keep a Moorish villa on the island, have shot many campaigns there. Ibiza has become a muse, just like Loulou de la Falaise or Betty Catroux. But Jagger was there early, and she can take some credit for nudging the island back onto the style map.

What most people do not realize about Ibiza is that all the touristy mega-clubs—Amnesia, Pacha, Space (which doesn't open until five in the morning), and the ten-thousand-person-capacity Privilege, billed as the "largest club in the world"—are clumped together on the southern side. Jagger went off the well-traveled path, to the north coast, and rediscovered an Ibiza that looked as it always had: Rolling pine forests dotted with rustic Spanish farms, citrus orchards, and a few grazing sheep.

Previous pages: Jade Jagger and her brood pile onto a bed in one of her guest tepees on the Spanish isle of Ibiza.

A hippie flea market at Las Dahlias in San Carlos has off-the-grid travelers selling wares collected on recent trips to Turkey, Senegal, or India. On certain nights there is a dance party done up in Indian pinks and oranges, with little kiosks selling chai and carrot cakes, just like in Goa, where a good number of the revelers have undoubtedly spent the winter.

Jagger's house, a five-hundred-year-old finca, is set apart from the whirl. It's just outside the innocent little village of Sant Joan: A charming mix of the traditional—terra-cotta tile and white-washed walls—and the modern (there is an all-organic pizza place). Jagger's compound is a similar example of the traditional-modern mix, including architectural and decorative references that could be mistaken for conventional were they not also adorned with playful, idiosyncratic touches.

The powder-pink swimming pool on the terraced hillside has canvas-canopied daybeds to match. It looks like a vintage Slim Aarons photo of the Monte Carlo Beach Club until you notice the giant disco ball suspended over the water between two palm trees. A pair of tepees have been arranged near an organic garden for overflow houseguests, such as Kate Moss or the fashion designer Matthew Williamson, both of whom inevitably wander through during the summer.

The farmhouse proper is wall-to-wall white minimalism, but ethnic collectibles relax the mood: Textiles from India, vintage Moroccan chandeliers, and a collection of Ganeshas. To make the house party even more of a party, a deejay station with turntables and mixers has been placed under the old log ceiling, and a wall has been dedicated to displaying Jagger's collection of Warhols and Guy Bourdins.

But her bedroom is the real kicker. To get in, Jagger and her boyfriend, deejay Dan Williams, have to step through a giant circle that recalls a Studio 54 bangle. They sleep on a round bed in the middle of the room, under a vintage tasseled canopy decorated with a papal seal—a canopy that was once used by Spanish cardinals as a sun shield.

Occasionally, Jagger, who is a pretty good deejay in her own right, will spin some tunes at her weekly party, Jezebel, held at various nightclubs around the island. Up north, she's down home. But she's still a celebrity. Recently, the paparazzi caught her sunbathing nude on a beach near her house. She didn't have any tan lines.

SEAN GULLETTE YTO BARRADA

In the blast of white, sun-bleached Tangier afternoons, the American actor and filmmaker Sean Gullette likes to set up in the lobbies of the city's grand-dame hotels and write. Depending on his mood, he might go to the Hotel Continental, an old whitewashed dowager down by the port that recalls a decadent past, or maybe El Minzah, with its 1970s ersatz Hispano-Moorish decor. If he feels like taking a swim after work, he'll go to the modern Hôtel Club Le Mirage, which is carved into a rocky cliff and has powerful views of the Atlantic and a private beach with a desolate charm in the off-season.

Above: Sean Gullette attempts a Moroccan mandolin at the Sons of Strait rehersal space in Tangier. *Right:* The couple with their baby, Vega, and pet donkey beneath their tree house.

صباح
MAGDA
SABAH
ROYALE SODIFILM Casablanca
1963
سينما الريف
CINEMA RIF
1,00
1,60

Gullette and his wife, Yto Barrada, ended up in Tangier as a result of fate more than choice. Gullette, who cowrote and starred in *Pi,* an experimental film directed by his Harvard classmate Darren Aronofsky, had been living in Manhattan for fifteen years and was "craving a patch of green." He had started hanging out in a community garden in the East Village called El Jardín del Paraíso when Barrada, a photographer who was brought up in Morocco but living in Paris, came to New York for her exhibition at the International Center of Photography. She appeared in the garden and amid the reeds, saw Gullette lounging in a lawn chair, and inquired about the very unusual octagonal tree house perched in a giant willow. The tree house had been built for the neighborhood kids by Gullette's friend Roderick Romero.

Jump a few years into the future: It's 2004, and Barrada decided to put into motion a plan she's had ever since visiting her mother in Tangier a couple of years earlier, when she'd happened upon the run-down Cinema Rif, an art deco movie theater in the city's main market square, the Grand Socco. She envisions this theater as a new cultural center, showing quality North African, Arabic, and international films. Gullette, exhausted by the "little square gray shopping-mall-slash-nightclub," as he calls it, that Manhattan had become for him, practically jumped on the next flight out.

Almost as soon as they touched down on the palm-lined tarmac, the couple were elbow-deep in the arduous renovation of the peeling 1938 theater—a beautiful rotting shell that, Gullette says, once "played old Bollywood movies subtitled in three languages, all scratched up, to about a dozen unemployed men who walked in late and talked loudly all through it."

They dusted off the colorful geometric Moorish tiles and created a state-of-the-art theater. Barrada renamed it Cinémathèque de Tanger and opened it two years ago as what is possibly the first and only art house in North Africa. Now it's a catalyst for the city's cultural scene. In the evenings revelers gather in the airy café, decorated with vintage photos of Moroccan movie stars, and outside at the fountains beside next to the stately facade, which looks like retro South Beach crossed with the medina.

In the 1940s and '50s Tangier was a lawless international zone with free-flowing drugs, rampant homosexuality, and tolerance for late-night romantic intrigue. Holding court were writers like William S. Burroughs and Paul Bowles, who lived there until his death in 1999. Woolworth heiress Barbara Hutton resided in a sprawling palazzo, Sidi Hosni, where she hosted outlandish costume parties with flamenco dancers and movie stars. Fashion designer Yves Saint Laurent lived nearby. French philosopher Bernard-Henri Lévy still keeps a summer villa near the center of town, which has been given a starkly contemporary face-lift by interior designer extraordinaire André Putman. It's next door to the legendary Café Hafa, where men in fezzes and slippers lounge on shaded terraces in plastic chairs, sipping thick, sugary mint tea and puffing on kif. These days the city is more of a design attraction than a literary one, with decorators, architects, landscapers, fashion designers, photographers, and artists trickling over from Europe to renovate palazzi on the cheap.

Previous pages: A 1963 photo shows a boy lounging next to a fruit stand in the Old Medina with an advertisement for the Cinema Rif, the theater that Gullette and Barrada converted into the art house Cinémathèque de Tanger.

Gullette and Barrada live in a modernist cement house on Old Mountain, the ritzy section of town just outside the casbah. There, palatial colonial villas with fortress-style doors stretch out on winding roads that overlook the Strait of Gibraltar. When the couple bought their house, it was a complete mess and had no electricity or running water. They gave it a top-to-bottom renovation, adorning the space with antiques they plucked from local flea markets. With old interlocking French wooden shutters, they converted their derelict greenhouse into a loftlike family room.

An enormous black fig tree in their backyard hosts the giant, boat-shaped tree house. It was built by their friend Roderick Romero, who they had invited over to conduct a tree-house-building workshop for local kids assisted by Darna, a charity for disadvantaged children. The project was made possible by donations from Romero's yogic clients including Sting, Donna Karan, and Russell Simmons. Gullette heads the 212 Society, a nonprofit that helps raise money for Tangier charities. His cochair is English model Jacquetta Wheeler, a Tangier regular whose villa has been in the family for three generations.

Gypsetters to the core, Gullette and Barrada (and now their young daughter Vega Violet) can be found jetting between Brazil, Mexico, Barcelona, Stockholm, and Paris for work and play, staying with their expansive network of creative friends everywhere they go. A 1985 Range Rover that Gullette finagled from a customs seizure is being souped up for off-road family trips around Morocco and North Africa.

When Gullette and Barrada are not traveling, their days start early with yoga sessions in the tree house and might end at a social event thrown by a member of Tangier's eccentric expat community. "Being in a major city can rub the rough edges off people," says Gullette. "But when you get a little more space between people, like in Tangier, their eccentricities can flourish." Socializing in Tangier, as is customary throughout Morocco, often takes place behind closed doors. In the summer, boozy garden fetes are held in old palazzi straight out of the "lord of the manor" era. White-gloved waiters serve *pastille* of pigeon, and bartenders mix gin and tonics for an ascot-wearing and tipsy crowd. It was at one of these parties, which often extend late into the evening, that Gullette heard a gossipy tale of the city told in accents from England, Italy, France, and points farther away. Apparently, Barbara Hutton, while in her late forties and living in Tangier, fell in love with a twenty-three-year-old musician who played piano at Dean's Bar. Eventually, the young pianist fell in love with a British girl his own age, and they moved away from Hutton—and into the house where Gullette and Barrada now live. The story inspired Gullette's latest film, *The Americans.* To Gullette, Tangier's dilapidated and illicit charm seems like an entity in itself, on par with William Burroughs or Paul Bowles. He doesn't for a second miss the "Richard Simmons–like state of overexcitement" of his old life in New York City.

"GULLETTE AND BARRADA LIVE IN A MODERNIST CEMENT HOUSE ON OLD MOUNTAIN, THE RITZY SECTION OF TOWN JUST OUTSIDE THE CASBAH. THERE, PALATIAL COLONIAL VILLAS WITH FORTRESS-STYLE DOORS STRETCH OUT ON WINDING ROADS THAT OVERLOOK THE STRAIT OF GIBRALTAR."

A typical Tangier courtyard featuring Moorish architecture and a reflecting pool surrounded by Morrocan tiles at the home of Italian writer, botanist, and landscape designer Umberto Pasti.

Opposite: An English wing chair, Moroccan textiles, and a sea view create an idyllic setting for afternoon tea atop Gullette and Barrada's treehouse.

NICOLAS MALLEVILLE

The most exciting night in Valladolid, a sleepy Spanish colonial town in the parched interior of the Yucatán peninsula in Mexico, is Sunday, when a band sets up in the evening under the stone arches of the Ayuntamiento, or city hall, and jam on traditional *jaranas.* The days are scorching hot, but there are Spanish tiles in Gothic mansions to keep your toes cool and large, stately palms for catching shade. It seems like the last place on Earth for an in-demand, male model to be based, but this is where Nicolas Malleville lives: in a two-room apartment above his perfumery with his Italian girlfriend.

Malleville's flawlessly chiseled jaw is a regular feature of campaigns for Gucci, Burberry, Armani Exchange, and DKNY. He can often be seen barreling out of town, past the imposing Cathedral of San Gervasio, toward the international airport in Cancún to jet off for assignments. (Malleville likes to point out that you can get direct flights from Cancún to almost anywhere.) A recent week had him displaying his

Above: A guest room in the 500-year-old Spanish villa that Nicolas Malleville converted into a perfumery, spa, and inn.

Opposite: Malleville and his Italian girlfriend, Francesca Bonato, in their bedroom in Valladolid.

masculine pout on the coconut-strewn shores of Santorini, Capri, and Madeira. "It's sort of like being a fireman," he muses. "They tell you where to go, and you get there as quick as you can." Malleville is on his cell phone, and his voice is breaking up. As usual, he's out in the desert, trolling for agave and citronella for his scent lab.

Modeling is great for paying the bills, but Malleville would much rather be in the Yucatán, expanding his homegrown empire, Coqui Coqui, a business that includes only things that look, smell, and taste good: a café and perfumery in Valladolid, a guesthouse near the Mayan ruins in Coba, and an inn of seven rooms on the beach in Tulum. If Buckminster Fuller could dream up an architectural utopia, then why can't Malleville create one for the senses? Being a male model shouldn't disqualify one from being Gypset. After all, one of the great Gypset characters in film—albeit a parodic character—was a model named Hansel played by Owen Wilson in *Zoolander.* The set of Hansel's SoHo loft was created by the talented interior-design duo Stephen Alesch and Robin Standefer, better known as Roman and Williams, who have a rad surf house of their own in Montauk, New York. Hansel's loft had orange-robed Tibetan houseguests, a skate ramp painted with a giant Hindi diety, a hot tub, and a tantric sex platform. But I digress.

Malleville, who has Basque, French, Italian, and Austrian blood, grew up on a sprawling ranch in Argentina's Pampas region, which is known for its cattle and rugged gauchos. As a teen he was obsessed with plants, and he studied landscape architecture at the local university before moving to Paris to take classes at the Bagatelle Gardens. It was there that he decided to supplement his nonexistent income by modeling. Star-making photographer Mario Testino cast him immediately for a J. Crew campaign, and from then on, Malleville's career escalated nonstop.

He hopped around the fashion capitals, living for a while in London and New York City, and his life was a fast-paced blur of late nights and bright lights. He ended up in the Yucatán by accident. In 2001 a friend invited Malleville to join her there for her birthday. She wanted to drive to the gringo party metropolis of Cancún, but Malleville wisely persuaded her that it would be better to explore the peninsula's small towns, which are rich in Mayan ruins. He had read about the history of the Yucatán's flora and scents. Apparently, the Franciscan monks, with the help of the Mayans, had gathered and chronicled the aromas of local tropical flowers, spices, woods, and exotic herbs for Spanish royalty.

When Malleville set eyes on Tulum, he was so seduced by the vegetation that he plunked down $170,000 for a swatch of land on the Caribbean beachfront. He built a rambling, group-size stone house with a palm-thatched roof and began distilling his own perfume. Houseguests started showing up by the planeload. The only way Malleville could afford to float the party was

Previous pages: The dining perch of Coqui Coqui, Malleville's inn in Tulum, Mexico (left). A laid-back suite with a hammock overlooking the Atlantic Ocean (right).

to convert the tropical getaway into a small inn—a very Gypset way of making things work. He took bits of inspiration from his favorite corners-of-the-world hotels; the Adrere Amellal Egypt's Siwa Oasis on the border of Libya; the Begawan Giri in Ubud, Bali; and the Hacienda Uayamon, a 19th century wood-dye factory turned sisal plantation in Compeche, Mexico.

Malleville's inn has a no-frills alt-luxury aesthetic meant to appeal to those whose idea of a five-star accommodation is a room that features actual stars and a clear ocean, kitted out with high-thread-count sand. Guests must make do without the Internet or air-conditioning, and they have only intermittent access to electricity and cell-phone reception. The rooms are furnished with handmade crafts Malleville commissioned from local artisans: hammocks, straw baskets, cotton bedspreads, and little else. "Traveling so much, you miss the warm parts of home," says Malleville, who imported his girlfriend, Francesca Bonato; his sister Coni; his cousin Julieta; and even his former Argentine nanny, Silvy, to staff the operation.

A five-hundred-year-old building on the Street of the Friars in the tiny town of Valladolid, about one hundred miles southwest of Cancún, is the current nexus of Malleville's empire. "The town is sleepy and undiscovered," he says, describing Valladolid as an "anti–San Miguel de Allende." In other words, the town provides the perfect raw material for an up-and-coming Gypsetter such as Malleville. His first move was to give his dilapidated building a minimalist-conquistador makeover and move in upstairs. Now it's a perfumery, laboratory, and spa. Two guest rooms are furnished with antiques that came from local mansions: a baroque gold-and-crystal chandelier and a carved wooden princess bed. Needless to say, there are no kitschy paintings of sunsets or seagulls on the adobe walls. In fact, the only ornamentation is the ancient palm ceiling beams and a dark border painted on the centuries-old stone floor. (For the overflow guests Malleville recently acquired another old villa nearby that he's converting into a larger inn.)

Malleville says the Yucatán is very cosmopolitan "in an unexpected way," with "collages of people" from Mexico, Italy, the United States, France, and England. "The Yucatán is becoming more and more like the center of the world for me," he says. And soon it may be the center for many others. He persuaded Kenyan adventuress Carolyn Roumeguere, a fellow Gypsetter (see page 134), to buy a house down the street. And it seems that more of his modeling clients are traveling to Mexico to work with him, as opposed to the other way around. Maybe they just want an excuse to hang out in the Yucatán. But that's how these communities always begin.

DAMIEN HIRST AND MAIA NORMAN

Above: Damien Hirst and Maia Norman's houseboat moored on the Thames River, London.

Opposite: Norman on the deck with her seafoam-colored longboard.

The biggest, richest, and most controversial art star of the new century is Damien Hirst. He's the bad boy to end all bad-boy artists, and is best known for putting dead and sometimes rotting animals inside giant glass tanks. In 2008, the peak year of his fame to date, he sold more than $300 million worth of his work.

Hirst has redefined the art world and made it work on his own idiosyncratic terms. When he was just out of Goldsmith's art college and setting up renegade gallery shows of his and his friends' work in semi-abandoned warehouses outside central London, he said, on the record, "I can't wait to get into a position to make really bad art and get away with it." He was only half joking. His art is often a conceptual flirtation with commerce, like *The Golden Calf,* a bull in formaldehyde with eighteen-cart gold hooves and horns that he

Yater

"WHEN IN LONDON, HIRST AND NORMAN STAY ON A HOUSEBOAT NOT FAR FROM CHELSEA BRIDGE. IT'S NOT SO MUCH A PIED-À-TERRE AS A PIED-À-MER. THOUGH YOU CAN HARDLY SURF THE THAMES, A BEACH THEME PREDOMINATES. SHELVES AND TABLES ARE DECORATED WITH SOUVENIRS FROM THE COUPLE'S TRAVELS TO EXOTIC, OFF-THE-BEATEN-PATH PLACES."

An afternoon snack served on deck.

Opposite: Norman's handpicked art collection, colorful pillows, and high-gloss planks update the standard nautical theme.

created for his controversial Sotheby's sale in September 2008, where he sold directly to buyers without using a gallery. When the market crashed a month later he actually seemed amused: "I think it's quite good (adjustment in art market prices) because it became unreal..." Hirst told the *Independent*. "You start to think you are touched by God. I have always thought that art is worth what the next guy is prepared to pay."

Hirst is a self-made mogul, but you would never catch him sporting designer-logo loafers or hanging out in the same trendy resorts as many of his oligarch patrons. He and his partner, Maia Norman, a surfer and fashion designer from California, have crafted a lifestyle that has completely subverted the concepts of luxury and a prestigious address. When in London, they stay on a houseboat not far from Chelsea Bridge. It's not so much a pied-à-terre as a pied-à-mer. Though you can hardly surf the Thames, a beach theme predominates. The knobs on the kitchen drawers were made to look like bits of sea-worn driftwood. Shelves and tables are decorated with souvenirs from the couple's travels to exotic, off-the-beaten-path places: Reindeer horns, bones, bowls from Africa. The walls are lined with portraits of Native Americans of the Pacific Northwest and the surfing Calhoun sisters of California's Topanga Canyon, as well as a reminder of wilder days past: A picture of Hirst waving his willy at the camera.

Norman has definitely been an instrumental Gypset influence. She grew up on the beach in Orange County and was a sponsored bodysurfer in her teens. She spent the seventies as a Southern California punk, graduating to the postpunk scene in Paris and London in the eighties. She supported herself selling jewelry and amused herself cruising the art world. She never missed an opening and soon became something of a fashion icon on the scene. A typical outfit might have been black tights modified with the tip of her burning cigarette, a vintage dress from the fifties, kitten heels, and a horsehair necklace of her own design. Norman and Hirst met in 1989 and were instantly drawn to each other's willingness to shun conventional life in favor of a self-created one.

"When I met [Hirst], he had a mattress on the floor of a rented room in a council block. He taught me to bake bread and lure a spider out of its web with live flies. We talked about art and books and nonsense, and, best of all, he made me laugh," Norman recalls. "We drank up quite a storm together." The nineties were a decade of cocaine, alcohol, and riotous excess. Hirst's shock-the-bourgeoisie fame started feeding on itself. The couple's nights together began to include people like Miuccia Prada, Elizabeth Hurley, and Elton John. Hirst would load up, go out on the town in London, and pull down his trousers for the paparazzi. Norman would join in the antics. For them, it seemed like a kind of performance art.

It was a lot of fun, but after the birth of their first child, Connor, Norman took the family back to her beach-bum roots. They bought a former inn and farmhouse by the sea in remote Devon, in the southwest of England where there's an abundance of long, peeling waves. Their home is three hundred years old and built from stone yet is anything but stuffy. There is a kitchen garden outside, surfboards lean by the door, and inside is a riot of life. Besides three kids, the family now includes a sheepdog and nine cats. The house is full of toys, art, and Mexican blankets. The hundred acres of woods and field are dotted with monumental modern sculptures from Hirst's collection and crisscrossed with coastal paths. Sometimes Norman rides through them on her knobby-wheeled dirt bike. The kids ride quads. She describes summers there as "the California dream without the freeways."

Winters are spent in a beach house near Zihuatanejo, Mexico, a town that became notorious in the early sixties as the site of an LSD commune founded by Timothy Leary and coconspirator Richard Alpert. After being fired from Harvard, Leary and his entourage rented out the town's sole hotel, the Catalina. Each morning would begin with a dose of liquid LSD. Then Leary would guide the tripping communards with readings from The Tibetan Book of the Dead. The experiment lasted six weeks, until the authorities shut it down. Hirst and Norman discovered the area in the mid-nineties: A place that could combine Norman's passion for surfing with Hirst's for art. (Another art-world Gypsy king and surfer, Julian Schnabel, recently bought a house nearby.) "I suppose the whole thing is really death," Hirst has said, explaining Mexico's appeal. "In England people hide or shy away from death and ideas about it, whereas Mexicans walk hand in hand with it." But then death started getting a little too close, even for Hirst. Several shark attacks, including one that killed a surfer, occurred off the main beach near their house. So for that reason or others, in typical Gypset fashion, Hirst and Norman spun the globe—metaphorically—and are now considering a move to the sands of Indonesia.

THE MIGNOT SISTERS

Above: Palapa roof, bongo drums, and a daybed covered in embroidered quilts and pillows.

Opposite: Nathalie and Sophie Laurence Mignot scope the surf from the roof of thier lair in Sayulita, Mexico, modeling black pearl necklaces and tie-dyed miniskirts of their own design.

I found the Mignot sisters—Nathalie, Sophie Laurence, and Marie José—half by accident and half by rumor, which, of course, is the perfect way to meet a Gypsetter. They're notorious up and down the coast of Mexico, on Saint Barts, and around the South Pacific. If you see a black-pearl necklace strung with leather and carelessly tied around someone's neck, you know they have encountered "the sisters" and have a story to tell. The necklace is not just any piece of jewelry; it's a secret sign of belonging, sort of like a kabbalah string or a gang tattoo.

The whole family has serious Gypset credibility. They are nine brothers and sisters (Richard, Yvan, Marie José, Anne, Marc, Jean-Noel, Nathalie, Sophie Laurence, and Christophe.) Some were born in France and others in Africa. Their parents, Marie-Vonna and Gerard, raised the family in Europe, Canada, and the Caribbean, eventually settling in Saint Barts, before it became overrun with private jets and real estate tycoons.

La vie
est Belle

At some point along the way, the kids decided it would be a grand adventure to buy a seventy-five-foot wooden boat, paint it the Rasta colors of red, gold, and green, and sail around the world. For the next decade they did just that, coming ashore for months at a time in little villages and remote patches of sand in Colombia, Venezuela, Costa Rica, and Panama. Along the way the Mignots accumulated girlfriends, boyfriends, and several kids, so they expanded their bohemian navy to three sailboats, becoming a sort of nautical Gypsy caravan cruising the oceans in search of good surf and secluded beaches.

While the brothers sailed on, a handful of the sisters came ashore in Sayulita, Mexico, a fishing village turned dropout paradise on the Pacific coast, an hour or so north of Puerto Vallarta. They turned an old, run-down building into a matrilineal lair overlooking the best surf break in town.

With its mellow vibe, Sayulita has become a quaint slacker enclave over the past few years, a Gypset equivalent to Acapulco. There are too many smoothie stands and postcollegians clogging the beach, but with its soft sea and banana-leaf shade, the place is inherently charming. The small town center is lined with brightly painted bodegas, fish-taco stands, yoga-surf camps, and myriad cafés, all of them packed with barefoot surfers sipping postsession cappuccinos. At night

Nathalie, Lola, Cha Cha, Sophie Laurence, and Elliot Mignot on the beach in Sayulita. Nathalie and Sophie Laurence wear their interpretations of the traditional Mexican wedding dress.

the local rancheros ride their horses through the streets and expats get drunk on tequila at candlelit bars. At one of them I meet a Carlos Castaneda disciple from Croatia who has been munching peyote and walking around Mexico barefoot for the past decade—a typical lotus-eating Sayulita acolyte.

The Mignot sisters settled down in 2003 with their collective brood of children, upstairs from their boutique, Pachamama. The store feels less an overt moneymaking enterprise than an extended parlor where information is traded about coming storm swells and the previous night's tequila-fueled hookups. The merchandise is a wearable travelogue. There is a sexier reworking of the traditional Mexican wedding dress, embroidered by a family of weavers in Chiapas. The leather miniskirts are crafted in León, a town on the coast near Guadalajara. And pullover beach shirts woven with disco-gold thread come from their travels to India. Trying on the clothes, you get the feeling they've come right out of the sisters' closets. Most likely they did, which, if you've fallen under the sisters' spell, makes them even more covetable.

The greatest treasures are the Tahitian black pearls. The Mignots discovered them on one of their sailing trips across the South Pacific.

"The pearls vibrate on the same frequency as love. When you are in love, everything is shiny," says Sophie Laurence. "They have this effect. They don't like chlorine; they respond poorly to things that aren't pure. We should be like them."

My mind flashes to Todos Santos, near the tip of Baja California, where I first glimpsed the gleaming pearls, around the neck of a very hot blond surfer from New York City. I saw the jewels flash again on the tanned arms of a woman I met down the coast from Puerto Vallarta, at the surreal resort Costa Careyes. When I told her I was heading north to Sayulita, she dialed up Nathalie. "Sí! Sí! Gracias!" she said into the phone, and then to me, "They are expecting you."

Just like that. I eventually found the Mignots' compound down a side street by the beach. When I walked upstairs, I saw an international crash pad that puts most boutique hotel designers to shame. The sisters did the renovation themselves, on the cheap, tricking it out with references to sailboats, Mexican architect Luis Barragán's bright palette, and Thor Heyerdahl's *Kon-Tiki*. It's not about money, after all; it's about taste and off-the-grid references. (And, of course, it helps if you're French, as they are.)

Once settled in Sayulita, I joined a couple of surfers lounging in the hammocks under a big palm-thatched *palapa* roof, in an area that doubles as a makeshift living room. Gangs of little bleached-blond kids swish past like extras from *Dogtown* and *Z-Boys*, boxing one of the hanging punching bags. I'm told to help myself from the rack of surfboards—a rare gesture among surfers, who are generally possessive of their fleet.

Previous pages: Mexican embroidered pillows and straw mats overlooking Sayulita's main surf break (left). The Mignot clan gathers in their compound (right).

That night blenders whirl in the kitchen with fresh mango margaritas and dinner is served around a big wooden table with traditional Mexican Equipale chairs covered in fuchsia leather. The chairs clash perfectly with the walls, which are painted in bright Mexican reds. Little altars hold Virgin effigies and lots of candles. "We added the candles originally because the electrician didn't show up for months," says Nathalie.

The sisters show me the bedrooms, which are stacked in two levels with shutters between them instead of walls. On the upper level an assortment of rash guards and bikinis hang over the railing. Nathalie leads me to one of the rooms but tells me they don't really belong to anyone, explaining, "It's sort of a first-come-first-served basis."

I find this out the hard way one night when I party with the sisters. We dress up in floppy hats and long, beaded necklaces from their shop and hit the bars—including a very strange, French-Moroccan-themed one that serves absinthe—and literally end up dancing in the streets. I'm the last one on the floor at an open-air club on the beach with a deejay spinning *cumbia* remixes. When I get back to the Mignots', all of the rooms are taken. So I crash on the only cushioned surface left, a canopied Balinese daybed set up on the deck with a cute guy already in it. When I squeeze in, he introduces himself as an "elf" from Washington State. The elves, he explains to me in a conversation that lasts until the sun begins to rise, are part of a do-it-yourself punk crafts movement in the Pacific Northwest.

It's very Gypset to take in wayward travelers, but surely there must be some criteria. I ask the sisters about this the next morning. "Yes, they must be *guapo*," jokes Nathalie. "They should bring happiness and joy. If they're coming from Italy, then they should bring a nice bottle of wine."

I easily decide to postpone my departure another week. We spend a fantastic Monday driving up the coast to a secret beach where we have a picnic and cover ourselves in a thick mud that the sisters assure me is restorative.

At first it seemed as though the sisters didn't do much more than a lot of partying and hanging out, but after a while I realized that they actually work very hard. It just doesn't seem like work. They are constantly sewing and making patterns in their home atelier—at least, when no one is sleeping in it. And they're always jaunting to Tahiti or India to collect more wares. It's hard to imagine the sisters living in a conventional city. They're so feral and spontaneous that I would worry about them getting arrested for speeding or nibbling at the take-out counter before the food was weighed. Sophie Laurence says these sorts of clashes with the everyday happen to her all the time whenever she reenters the real world—reason enough to stay in the sisters' handcrafted utopia.

DEVENDRA BANHART

Topanga Canyon, on a ridge stretching up the beach near Malibu, is the Gypset's Riviera. It's one of the original centers of the California brand of bohemianism, along with Big Sur and Bolinas, with roots that travel far deeper than the sixties. Neil Young recorded *After the Gold Rush* here, and it's where the young psychedelic singer-songwriter Devendra Banhart can be found in his funky little wooden house—when not on tour, that is.

Banhart, with kohl-rimmed eyes and long, unruly hair that he occasionally tucks into a colorful turban, is a formidable Gypsetographer. Every chunky ring piled on his fingers, bit of henna tattooed on the backs of his hands, and poem or drawing tacked to his wall has some sort of macro-travel story attached to it. Generally, it involves some combination of Native Americans, musicians from Mali, and Greek goddesses. Banhart's references are so far-flung and deep that he could never be accused of copping a cliché hippie look from the corner secondhand clothing shop. Consider his trippy music video for his song "Carmensita"—a mash of global references—in which Banhart stages a tipsy, jet-lagged version of a Bollywood film. His bare chest is covered with more necklaces and oversize beads than a maharaja's as he dances around in genie pants, singing in Spanish to his Indian princess (and now ex-girlfriend), Natalie Portman. In the background a posse of dancers in Nehru jackets and penciled-on Salvador Dalí mustaches follow the up-tempo beat.

Karl Lagerfeld was so impressed with Banhart's brand of tarted-up pan-culturalism that he invited the singer to perform by the runway at the Chanel fashion show in 2005. *The New York Times*, meanwhile, hailed him as a fabulous cross-dresser. (Banhart frequently sports lingerie and glimmering eye shadow.) But none of this would have been possible without a wanderlust-fueled imagination and an upbringing to match.

His parents were followers of the Indian child guru Prem Rawat. Now relatively obscure, Rawat was once the leader of the world's fastest-growing spiritual organization. As a six-year-old child, Rawat was was considered by many to be an incarnation of God. In the early seventies, at age thirteen, the holy child traveled to America and established a peace-and-love cult that at its peak had six million adherents worldwide, fifty thousand of them hippies in the United States—including Banhart's parents. After their baby was born (in Houston, in 1981) they took the still-nameless infant to be blessed by Rawat. He named the Banhart boy Devendra after the Hindu god of rain and thunder.

Banhart's parents eventually split, and he moved with his mom to Caracas, Venezuela, where he began listening to calypso, highlife, and *mento.* But the biggest influence was *tropicalismo*, a Brazilian blend of bossa nova, rock, and native music that had started in the sixties in response to the brutal military coup of 1964. The idea was that the free mixing of sounds—and cultures—could create something exciting, modern, and beautiful. The military dictatorship thought otherwise, labeling *tropicalismo* a decadent corrupter of youth and jailing its practitioners.

Banhart ended up at the San Francisco Art Institute, but even a progressive art school seemed too conventional. "I found myself ditching school and writing songs," he said, "that seemed, I don't know . . . more possible." He missed the combination of art, danger, travel, and esoteric knowledge

Previous pages: Gypset bard: Banhart poses with a tattooed chest, necklaces, and acoustic guitar.

that was once his world, and so off he wandered. He traveled to New York, Paris, and Asilah, an ancient seaside resort just outside Tangier. Along the way he wrote songs, recording them by calling a friend back in California and singing them into his answering machine, giving instructions that they should not be erased.

Banhart landed back in New York, crashing on couches and futons, exhibiting his drawings in little Lower East Side galleries, and releasing a torrent of music recorded on the well-respected Young God label. "Freak folk," the critics called it, putting Banhart at the center of a scene of extremely talented second-generation Gypsetters, including CocoRosie, Joanna Newsom, and Sufjan Stevens.

"If there's anyone we relate to, it's our moms and dads, and older hippies, people into Eastern philosophies and new age, in the sense that if you look at the seed of every religion, it's all the same, so let's start our own vague one based on love and peace and unity and going within. I suppose we like that kind of hippie as opposed to the white-dreaded, Hacky Sack–playing Dave Matthews hippie," Banhart told *The New York Times* after one of his concerts.

Banhart's home in Topanga reflects his view: There are carnival masks from the eighties, a jewelry studio housing doves made of bones, and portfolios of his primitive, folky drawings. Oh, and Jim Morrison's couch is in the living room. (Morrison lived nearby during the original hippie era, along with Joni Mitchell and Van Morrison, not to mention Charles Manson.)

When Banhart recorded his breakthrough album, *Smokey Rolls Down Thunder Canyon*, in 2007, the house was populated with a new generation of musicians, who have coalesced around him to create their own *tropicalismo*: California's hippie-folk past spiced with sounds from around the world. During the three months of recording, the house hosted an ever-changing roster of Gypset kids. They'd hear about the scene, hitchhike across the country with barely more than their mandolin or kalimba (an African thumb piano) and find the house just when their musical input was needed. When the day's session would end—usually at about three in the morning—a dozen people would crash among the batiks and Persian rugs, on the couch, in hammocks, in a circus tent set up in the backyard. Banhart called the scene "the family" and the music they made together "naturalismo." It was one big creative commune, and the door was always open to those who could hear the call.

ALICE TEMPERLEY

British fashion designer Alice Temperley is legendary not only for her eponymous collection but for her parties. She throws a weekend-long birthday bacchanalia every summer on her family's apple cider farm in Somerset, England. (Yes, the cider is alcoholic.) Hundreds of guests wander the country fields decked out in costumes—one year the theme was "Arabian Nights," another "Newcomers to Earth." A strange punch called "Love Potion Number Ten" is served, and things begin to spiral; revelers roll around in the apple orchard, dance barefoot in a bedouin tent, and tuck into the various Mongolian yurts and Indian tepees at dawn.

Above: Alice Temperley and a friend at Mad Hatters Tea Party. *Right:* Revelers arrive by stretch limo in a field of tepees for Temperley's summer birthday soiree in Somerset, England.

Temperley is one of London's most sought-after fashion upstarts. Stylish London girls—including her friends model Jacquetta Wheeler and actress Saffron Burrows—pine for her global-nomad Gypset wearables. She launched Temperley London in 2000 with her business partner and husband, Lars von Bennigsen, a former banker. Every season she sends loads of exotica down the runways: A harem-chic Oberon caftan tailored from billowy electric blue gauze, cut way up the thigh and way down the décolletage, seems destined for a courtyard in Riyadh or Marrakech; sexy khaki-hued camisoles and flirty safari dresses are perfect for a fireside dinner in a tent somewhere in the African bush. The point of each collection is to distill a wanderlust fantasy that's just the right balance of luxury and bohemia. It isn't a lot different from her real life.

Temperley's parents were what she calls "eccentric hippies." Growing up in Somerset, there were always houseguests, fresh from stopping over at the farm and sipping a steady flow of cider brandy. When the Temperley family went on a camping trip, it was via a horse-drawn Gypsy caravan. (This was all a little like Led Zeppelin's woodsy-Gothic period, but not as occult.) She attended her first of thirty Glastonbury music festivals at age three, and then the family was off to exotic lands. In Kenya they headed straight into the bush, without a guide, in an old beater of a car. Temperley spent all of her youthful travels obsessively collecting textiles, beads, masks—pretty much anything fashion-related that she could cart back home—and by the time she graduated from the University of London's Central Saint Martins College of Art and Design and the graduate program at the Royal College of Art, she had amassed thousands of fabric swatches from everywhere from India to Bali, along with an impressive collection of beads. Today beads and sequins are a Temperley trademark.

The designer still spends a lot of time in Somerset, sleeping in a tepee by a lake and experimenting with textiles. She's perfectly happy on the farm, using her parents' kitchen sink to dye alpaca sweaters crazy colors—a shocking fuchsia or a Moroccan cobalt blue—and then hanging them in the branches of the apple trees to cure the clothes in the sun. But she couldn't very well run a fashion empire from Somerset, so she brought Somerset to London. She and von Bennigsen bought up a row of mews on a sleepy cobblestone side street in Notting Hill to create an urban Gypset refuge. Some of the carriage houses were converted into Temperley's showroom; other buildings were turned into the couple's living quarters, to which they added another mews just before Alice got pregnant with their son, Fox London. "A lucky coincidence," says Temperley.

She flits about the rooms like a barefoot wood nymph, with an entourage of Pre-Raphaelite assistants and a shih tzu lapdog. Some parts of the compound recall a tree house, other parts a bohemian crash pad: Big arched doorways, a mounted moose head, a sleeping loft, and Gothic stained-glass windows.

Previous pages: The giving tree: Temperley sun cures her just-dyed dresses in the orchard with a little help from her friends.

Travel is Temperley's muse. She is constantly taking reconnaissance trips to Marrakech, Kerala, and Ibiza, where in the tradition of her youth, she loves to comb the souks and bazaars. Her jewelry collection was inspired by a trip back to the Kenyan bush: This time the family pitched tents under the moon and winged it from place to place in a run-down airplane. "The ultimate luxury is not a flashy five- or six-star resort," she says. "To me, travel is about raw experience and discovering the unexpected under the stars."

New Year's is often spent in Cuixmala, Mexico, an exclusive "estate-and-breakfast" owned by Temperley's friend and fellow Gypsetter Alix Goldsmith. A few hours south of Puerto Vallarta on the Pacific coast, Cuixmala was the brainchild of Alix's father, Jimmy Goldsmith, the late British billionaire financier and environmentalist. It's a biosphere reserve with more than thirty thousand acres, several small guest casitas, grazing antelope, and miles of private beach. On a cliff by the ocean is Jimmy's apocalypse-proof Indian-themed villa, which looks as if a considerate cyclone gingerly dropped it from Rajasthan on the edge of the Mexican jungle.

The whole stretch of coast has long been an eccentric Gypset enclave. On an island nearby there's a human-size nest built by Roderick Romero, the sculptor who created the Tangier tree house belonging to Sean Gullette and Yto Barrada (see page 88). Careyes, a resort a few miles north of Cuixmala, was started in the late 1960s by the Italian artist Gian Franco Brignone. It's another surrealistic leisure utopia where caftans and sarongs are prized over golf courses and yachts. Jimmy Goldsmith was one of Brignone's first guests. (Brignone's studio, two splayed rectangles painted sky blue, has a giant, rough-hewn wooden Jack and the Beanstock ladder in the center, leading way up toward the clouds. On one rectangular roof is a massive question mark laid out in rocks; on the other, an exclamation point.)

I happened upon the scene one warm starlit night while strolling on the beach a few years ago. A long table for forty was set up on the sand. The whole affair was lit by torches and sprinkled with bougainvillea. It was a secret party in the middle of paradise; Alix Goldsmith was the host. Temperley and the other guests, clinking margaritas and glasses of red wine, were a whirl of slender shoulders draped in shawls. Anyone who could find the party was invited. It was, I would discover, vintage Temperley.

CONSUELO CASTIGLIONI

While most fashion designers make the scene in Sardinia or the Hamptons, Marni's creative director, Consuelo Castiglioni, prefers to camp out on a cliff of jagged rocks on the teensy Spanish island of Formentera. There's no airport—she has to fly to Ibiza from her base in Milan and hop a small passenger ferry—and many of the roads are dirt. (The island was abandoned for almost three hundred years and used as a prison camp during Franco's regime.)

But slow down and you'll notice almond trees, grapevines, anise plants, bougainvillea, and a few goats wandering in the tall, prickly grass. Explore further, past the cactus gardens and fig orchards, and you'll eventually come

to the shore, a moonscape that juts into the dreamy blue Mediterranean. That is where one might find Castiglioni, chilling out inside a brown camel-skin bedouin tent she picked up on a trip to Kuwait. The designer's haute fort lacks creature comforts like air-conditioning or even a floor, but it has been given the same quirky-clever, high-low work-over that is the unmistakable signature of her runway collections.

Inside the tent fluffy white flokati rugs cover the ocher-colored rocks and keep toes safe from sharp corners. Chairs from tribal Afghanistan and African stools are mixed with seventies-style pod loungers. Outside, Castiglioni's creative approach to gardening could win a prize. Instead of doing any, she sprinkled silver pebbles and purple marbles over the parched and scrubby earth, and turned the rather hostile terrain into an open-to-the-elements Italian disco. It's the kind of landscape where a fashionable space alien would be thrilled to park her flying saucer.

Castiglioni's Gypset approach to life extends to her career as a fashion designer—or perhaps it's the other way around. She started her label on a whim, never intending for it to be more than a fanciful pastime. In the nineties her husband, Gianni, was running his family fur business in Milan, and Castiglioni couldn't bear the staid, semigeriatric shapes. So she decided to give the fur coats a youthful overhaul, leaving out the linings and dyeing them unusual hues. The pieces, many literally sketched out on envelopes under the racks, were such a success that her clients demanded she make some threads equally cool to wear beneath them. Despite the fact that Castiglioni never advertises or pushes her dresses on celebrities, her brand, with its quirky retro prints and surrealist proportions, has become the coveted favorite of the smart set: Everyone from the artist Cindy Sherman to the actress Maggie Gyllenhaal wears Marni.

Part of what makes the whole unlikely enterprise work is Castiglioni's Gypsy eye. She effortlessly mixes and layers unlikely prints and fabrics that are at once playful, sophisticated, and theatrical. The references are off the map, as is her jewelry, which looks like the result of a beachcombing stroll: She strings together stained glass, seed husks, and coconut shells in a souvenir-shop mash.

So it makes perfect sense that Castiglioni chose Formentera, where there are weekly markets and boutiques that sell reshaped Indian dresses and extra-flat straw sandals. Eccentricity is encouraged. After all, Formentera was home to both Pink Floyd and Bob Dylan in the 1960s. Walk inland from the nudist beaches, and you might happen upon a faux-medieval castle flying a German flag. And then there's Philippe Starck's self-designed beach house, which epitomizes no-frills chic. The experimental house is marked by low lines, huge cement staircases leading to the roof, primitive thatched palm awnings for shade, and small mattresses laid out on the terrace for catnaps. Castiglioni keeps a place inland, too, but she so loves the view that stretches out toward Africa that she and her husband are erecting a second perch near the bedouin tent. "There's no high-heel glamour here," she says. "Just sand and sun."

"PART OF WHAT MAKES THE WHOLE UNLIKELY ENTERPRISE WORK IS CASTIGLIONI'S GYPSY EYE. SHE EFFORTLESSLY MIXES AND LAYERS UNLIKELY PRINTS AND FABRICS THAT ARE AT ONCE PLAYFUL, SOPHISTICATED, AND THEATRICAL. THE REFERENCES ARE OFF THE MAP. . ."

Flokati shag rugs, 1970s-style pod chairs, and African tribal stools add a groovy flair to the rocky Mediterranean terrain.

Previous pages: Marni designer Consuelo Castiglioni, her husband Gianni, and their daughter, Carolina (center), relax in their Bedouin tent on the Balearic island Formentera.

ANDREA ZITTEL

The North American deserts from Southern California down to Mexico have long been considered the promised land for utopians, communards, outlaws, eccentric inventors, and nothing-to-lose homesteaders. And it is here at the fringes of the Mojave, in Joshua Tree, California, that we find the artist Andrea Zittel, a Gypsetter in repose. Consider Andrea's Escape Vehicles, aerodynamic stainless-steel mobile homes with no wheels. Beached in a garden or driveway, they provide "escape" when people climb inside, shut the door, and retreat into the custom interior. Escape Vehicles, like some of the artist's other work, suggest that the mad nomad barreling down the highway will eventually pull over on the side of the road to enjoy the view—and then stay for a spell.

Above: Andrea Zittel in her custom homesteader's cabin kitchen. *Opposite:* A metal "Wagon Station" guest cottage on Zittel's experimental living compound in Joshua Tree, California.

In 2000, Zittel, who has had major exhibitions at the Whitney Museum of American Art in New York and at the Museum of Contemporary Art in Los Angeles, decided to move her studio from a row house in Williamsburg, Brooklyn, to a parcel of parched land pocked with creosote

bushes, cactus, and lots of rocks. Why? "Because it seemed that one could do anything here," Zittel has said. Her twenty-five acres came with a charmless 1930s stucco cabin that she named A-Z West and turned into her home—or, as she describes it, "an institute for investigative living." She imported a few shipping containers, painted them gallery white, and set about constructing a playful personal utopia.

The old cabin has been revived into a pioneer's dream lair. Like a very hip RV, much of the house is retrofitted in birch paneling. The built-in wooden dinning table comes with bowls already carved into it. (She has since expanded the house to accomodate her growing ranks of friends and her son Emmett.) When Zittel was a child growing up in Southern California, her schoolteacher parents took the family on extended vacations in their Volkswagen camper and sailboat. "I sort of have a love-hate relationship with physically moving around so much," Zittel explains. "But I really do love the all-in-one interiors."

The living room is another testing ground. It reminds me of the polar bear cage at the zoo, but the hunks of gray foam that look like boulders scattered about are actually part of Zittel's Raugh furniture line. (I still haven't gotten over the shock of the Raugh exhibition at the Andrea Rosen Gallery in New York City a few years ago, in which naked models climbed around on the huge boulders like apes. Upon closer inspection, I realized that one of the squatting males was my copy editor.) "I like examining values and needs superimposed upon people by society. And I'm trying to figure how necessary they are and if there are other ways things could be," Zittel says.

Zittel's unconventional abode has a lot of precedents. Architectural utopians have a long history of geeking out in the desert. In the 1930s Frank Lloyd Wright built a live-by-example architecture school outside Scottsdale, Arizona, called Taliesin West. Students slept in experimental huts that they had designed in the desert out back. "I heard that Frank Lloyd Wright had his students arrive with a sleeping bag and a tuxedo," Zittel says. "The idea was that Wright would teach them polar-opposite skills: To be craftsmen and gentlemen. And they would leave being very well-rounded people." Paolo Soleri, an eccentric Taliesin alum from Italy, has tried to reach a higher plane of existence with Arcosanti, a planned eco-community that's been under construction in Arizona since the seventies.

Although art critic Jerry Saltz has described Zittel as a "gypsy-visionary, social-scientist, explorer-architect, eco-rogue, control-freak artist," she also seems to have a sense of humor about her enterprise, relishing the absurdity of her experiments with the everyday. How else might one explain her Interlopers hiking club? The IHC is a group of artists, friends, and local bons vivants who meet semiregularly to traipse around the Flintstone-esque landscape of the Mojave dressed in outrageous fashions: A Victorian brocade bodice and German knickerbockers, for example, or feathered chaps matched with a plumed riding helmet.

Fashion design, like interior design, is a key part of Zittel's ethos of "investigative living." After she graduated from the Rhode Island School of Design she worked as an archivist at Pat Hearn Gallery in New York City. Instead of stressing about expensive designer clothes, she made herself one black dress and wore it every day for six months. The idea inspired a line of boldly patterned minidresses in felted wool, crocheted knits, and holes. The designs have a stylish, comrade quality and work well layered over jeans and hiking boots. They remind me both of Prada and of Diane Keaton in Woody Allen's *Sleeper.* Zittel has modified fashion's seasonal rules, too. Who needs spring, resort, or fall collections? She picks one garment and wears it for the whole three months, which certainly makes getting dressed in the morning much breezier.

Experimental enclaves set up out of bounds are intrinsic to the Gypset philosophy. In Trinidad, for example, U.K. artists Peter Doig and Chris Ofili own a cinema society and exhibit in local galleries. The surrealists clustered in the remote Mexican town of Erongarícuaro, and the beats gathered in Tangier. Now Joshua Tree has become such a community, with artists including Ed Ruscha, Thom Merrick, and Jack Pierson, who likes to put the old roadside-sign letters he collects for his artwork out in the dirt behind his house to get that vintage sunbaked, look (see page 158).

"I'm interested in starting a node of energy outside of the cultural capitals," says Zittel. "Ideas move so quickly now, you almost need the filter of space."

Zittel, who jump-started the current desert art migration nearly a decade ago, has her own art happening, the High Desert Test Sites, an event in which artists make site-specific installations amid the boulders, caves, and cacti. (Past participants have included Mungo Thomson, Piotr Uklanski, and Leo Villareal.) Onlookers and revelers are given booklets with maps so they can track the whimsical creations in a wacky scavenger hunt that includes extracurriculars like stopping for hamburgers at cafés and dancing the electric slide at Pappy & Harriets, a local honky-tonk.

Not surprisingly, Zittel has a steady flow of guests, who often end up snoozing in her Wagon Stations, futuristic metal sleeping pods strewn about her yard. Each one is individually customized with painted hot-rod flames or hippie-bus wood panels on the outside. Inside each comes equipped with a camping stove, shelf, and sleeping mat. The pods (which are constantly being shipped off for museum exhibits, much to the dismay of guests) are meant as a double riff: A play on the Conestoga wagons of the western frontier as well as the station wagons of the suburban frontier.

But Zittel may have done too good a job of promoting the artistic frontier that she founded. The artist, who recently described herself as a "walking tourist attraction," lately has been thinking about turning A-Z West into a campground or foundation for other artists and heading farther out into the desert.

CAROLYN ROUMEGUERE

"I don't recall the sight of a goat or sheep being strangled ever shocking me, and would relish the warm blood straight out of the jugular vein in the same way I enjoy eating oysters in Lamu or buffalo mozzarella on the Amalfi coast." This is pretty much the prêt-à-porter mantra of Carolyn Roumeguere, a jewelry designer and adventuress who splits her time between Kenya and Mexico. Her mother was the famed French anthropologist Jacqueline Roumeguere-Eberhardt, a descendant of the cross-dressing Victorian-era explorer Isabelle Eberhardt (see page 60). Jacqueline spent a good deal of her time

Above: Roumeguere with daughter Cassia-Peia. *Right:* The view from her eucalyptus-wood deck at the designer's beach house on Lamu Island, Kenya.

"A REAL GYPSET SHANGRI-LA, THE TREE HOUSE, WHICH IS ACTUALLY A SERIES OF SMALL STRUCTURES WITH THATCHED ROOFS HELD UP BY ACACIA TREES, WAS CARVED OUT OF BIG WILD-OLIVE BRANCHES THEY FOUND AROUND THE PROPERTY."

Roumeguere and her son Dylan in their beach house in Lamu.

Opposite: The designer's bedroom in Kenya's Rift Valley, with mosquito netting canopy and Acacia branch trim.

Previous pages: A guest room in Roumeguere's Rift Valley tree house without doors or windows, only short walls made from fallen trees, held together with cement and red earth.

searching for hominids—elusive humanlike creatures said to live in Kenya's thick forests. On one expedition, she fell in love with her guide, a Masai tribesman. They married despite the rather astounding fact that he already had six wives. Young Carolyn was brought up among extended family in Kenya's Masai Mara National Game Park. Being raised in the bush has given her a unique perspective on life.

She zooms around Kenya behind the controls of a little 1954 Piper airplane with canvas wings that was originally sent to Kenya by the queen of England to help fight the Mau Mau. Romeguere affectionately calls it her "modern camel."

She met her husband, Simon Douglas-Dufresne, a third-generation Kenyan, because he sold her the plane. She had just crashed her Range Rover in the Masai Mara and decided that air travel would be safer. Marriage, flight lessons, and two kids followed soon after.

The mobile family now jumps between a town house in the Nairobi suburb of Karen, named after Danish writer Karen Blixen (better known as Isak Dinesen); a tree house on the edge of the Great Rift Valley in Kenya; a beach compound in Kenya's Lamu archipelago that looks straight out of *Robinson Crusoe;* and a seventeenth-century hacienda in Valladolid, a Spanish colonial village in Mexico's Yucatán. A lot of time is spent journeying from one place to the next, but, as Romeguere points out, "Distances mean nothing when time and space cease to exist as rigid entities. It's all an attitude of mind."

It's a fairly practical philosophy when you also consider her extensive business travel. The jewelry she makes, as globally referenced as herself, combines the modern with the tribal. She goes to India to find unique and intricate designs, to Ethiopia to collect crosses and silver beads, and to Yemen to gain inspiration from the bedouins. And then there's the matter of selling her wares, which she does by blowing into London and New York—wearing long, embroidered skirts, her arms clanking with exotic bangles and chains—and holding trunk shows. (Nicole Kidman, Kate Winslet, and Princess Caroline of Monaco are all customers.) Romeguere and her unique boho pieces, such as crosses made from cow horn and rubies, and pendants crafted from vintage *objets* like Dinka rings, are such an exotic attraction for city dwellers that she has become a muse to her friend Donna Karan, who frequently hosts the exclusive trunk shows.

But most crucial to Carolyn's art is her lifestyle. She stays clear of the overly trendy and obvious, not out of any concerted effort but from sheer genetic instinct. Without even thinking about it, she adheres to the unspoken Gypset rule of hanging out in places that are at least two to three hours from an international airport, preferably with a few dirt roads and ferries tossed in for good measure. Her island home on Manda, a patch of sand and ancient baobab and acacia trees a few minutes' boat-zoom from the Kenyan island of Lamu, is a perfect example. For Carolyn, Lamu, with

Arabic architecture and unspoiled, sprawling beaches, is an alternative to upscale vacation spots like Saint Barts or Saint-Tropez. There are few hotels, certainly no designer boutiques, and most of the action revolves around the bougainvillea-canopied terrace of the small, family-run Peponi, an inn where mysterious eccentrics mingle with fashion refugees and off-duty aristocrats.

Carolyn's perch is the coolest of all. Instead of some expat monstrosity—what artist Ashley Bickerton calls "dream architecture"—she prefers an old cottage on a jungly bit of African bush that Simon's grandparents bought in the 1960s from the sultan of Zanzibar. The couple amended it with a few big palm-thatched roofs that look like groovy sun hats and set a dining table on their beach. There's a large black snake that sleeps in the palm-log roof above their mosquito-net-canopied bed. "We leave it alone, and it does us no harm," Romeguere says. "After all, is it not he who is hosting us?"

To get to their tree house in the Kenyan part of the Great Rift Valley, Romeguere must fly the little plane over a massive waterfall that protects the house on one side and land on a homemade airstrip of dirt and sawdust-filled warthog holes. (The nearest village is a few hours' drive.) A real Gypset Shangri-la, the tree house, which is actually a series of small structures with thatched roofs held up by acacia trees, was carved out of big wild-olive branches they found around the property. There are no exterior walls to obstruct the 150-mile view that stretches all the way to Mount Kilimanjaro on a clear day, but inside the branches have been bent to frame everything from doorways to sinks, bookshelves, and mirrors, creating a wavy feeling that reminds Romeguere of Salvador Dalí's *montres molles*. A big copper bathtub that looks out over the valley is one of my favorite touches.

Mexico is a recent addition to the family's rotation. They went on holiday to the town of Valladolid, halfway between Cancún and Mérida, and fell in love with it. They met the model and hotelier Nicolas Malleville (see page 96) and his Italian girlfriend, who own a small inn and perfumery. The couple wanted to create a community of kindred spirits and suggested that Romeguere and Simon to buy a historic hacienda a few doors down from them. And, of course, they did.

MULANOVICH FAMILY

Punta Hermosa, a beach town about an hour south of Lima, Peru, possesses some of the best breaks east of Hawaii, as well as the house of the Mulanovich family: An unofficial inn for various Gypsetters on surf safari. I found myself there on a hot January morning.

Herbert and Ines Mulanovich are the patriarch and matriarch of the Peru surf scene. They are both old-school surfers. Their elder son, Herbert Jr., directs a surfing magazine, and Matias, the younger, is a pro surfer with a fabulous Afro. Sofía, their beautiful, blond middle child, became Peru's biggest celebrity after winning the surfing world championship in 2004. If you visit Peru, you'll see her smiling down at you from the giant billboards on the Pan-American Highway.

To find the Mulanoviches' house, I simply asked for directions from a crowd of tanned surfers walking down a dirt road with short boards under their buff arms. They pointed to a tall wooden gate that had no bell; another passerby with a short board pointed to a hanging conch shell

Above: Dusk in downtown Máncora, a small surf town in the north of Peru.

Opposite: The Mulanovich Family (Matias, Herbert Jr., Herbert Sr., Ines, and Sofía) at their home in Máncora, Peru.

"IT OCCURRED TO ME THAT SURFERS ARE GYPSET BY DEFAULT. EVERY TIME I TRAVEL TO SOME GROOVY COASTAL TOWN I FIND A HANDFUL OF CRAFTY SURFERS WHO HAVE GOTTEN THERE YEARS EARLIER. INVARIABLY, THEY'VE SET UP IN SOME AMAZING COMPOUND, TYPICALLY WITH LOTS OF PALM SHADE AND A VIEW OF THE BEST BREAK—A PLACE JUST LIKE THE MULANOVICHES'."

World champion Sofía Mulanovich gets ready to paddle out.

Opposite: The Mulanoviches hang out at the Mayan yellow pyramid camp, which belongs to their friend and architect José de Col. The pyramid sits on a cliff overlooking three of Máncora's best surf breaks.

and motioned for me to pull down on it. A parrot started squawking, and eventually Ines came to the door. She showed me to a bedroom that must have belonged to one of her kids and said I could stay as long as I liked. The two twin beds were made with superhero sheets, and the walls were plastered with surfing stickers. In the bathroom I found a defunct hot tub filled with short boards and wet suits. In the living room was a huge L-shaped couch where sinewy teens and sun-kissed surf pros intently watched surf videos play on the television. They were waiting for the next swell or for their cook to whip up ceviche and fried plantains—whichever came first.

I stepped outside and saw Herbert Jr. and Sofía scanning the ocean from the perfect vantage point of their backyard. Waves fanned out in all directions. Herbert Jr. pointed out Kontiki, a break with massive, untamed waves breaking far out to the side of an offshore reef that would have taken an arm much stronger than mine to paddle out to. During storms, Herbert Jr. said, Pico Alto, another brawny wave break, has a swell that can reach twenty-five feet in height.

"It's much less crowded than in Hawaii and California," said Sofía, who was slipping into her wet suit. "And even on the smallest day of the year, it's never flat."

It occurred to me that surfers are Gypset by default. Every time I travel to some groovy coastal town—from Todos Santos in Baja, Mexico to Guéthary in Basque country—I find a handful of crafty surfers who have gotten there years earlier. Invariably, they've set up in some amazing compound, typically with lots of leafy shade and a view of the best break—a place just like the Mulanoviches'.

Surfing has been a force in Peru ever since the 1930s, when playboy and socialite Carlos Dogny returned from Hawaii with a heavy wooden board given to him by Duke Kahanamoku, the father of modern surfing. In 1942 Dogny founded the elite Waikiki Surf Club in the Lima suburb of Miraflores, and since then, the country's ruling families have ridden the swells and gotten tipsy on Pisco sours in the clubhouse. The club still employs "board boys" who rush to the water's edge to carry and wax members' boards when they return from a session on the waves.

Both Ines and Herbert Sr. learned to surf at the Waikiki Surf Club, but in the eighties Lima became a fiery battleground as the Maoist group Shining Path warred with the government. Blackouts, car bombs, and assassinations were realities of daily life. Herbert and Ines bolted south, finding in Punta Hermosa a safe place to raise their children. The town has grown with the Mulanovich clan. It's now full of two-story concrete houses painted in tropical shades of green, blue, and red. But the Mulanoviches were among the first families to settle in the town, and their house is on a perch overlooking the peeling waves at a break called La Isla—a prep school for the pro surf circuit.

Ines explained to me that when Sofía was just a teen, she said that the ocean was her garden. "When other girls asked for dolls as gifts," said Ines, "she asked for surfboards."

Hanging around with Sofía in Punta Hermosa is like rolling with a rock star. She was the first Peruvian to become an international sports champion. She is a symbol of optimism after decades of economic woes, political repression, and terrorism. Every time she appears in a local contest, the beach is mobbed with people waving banners and cheering. (Her celebrity has its perks: During a jammed surfing event at Playa Roca—a wilder, South American version of Malibu—we got a plum parking space in return for her posing for a photo with the lot attendant.) These days Sofía is continually traveling to various competitions at the world's famed breaks, including Teahupoo in Tahiti, Hawaii's North Shore, and Australia's Byron Bay.

But she hangs out in Peru as much as possible. If the Mulanoviches hear of a big swell that's going to hit up the coast, they might hop a flight to Chicama, a town a few hundred miles to the north said to possess a point break with one of the longest rides in the world—if you jump on in the right place, it can last for almost a mile.

Máncora, a small fishing village near the southern border of Ecuador, is where the Mulanoviches go to really unwind. The area can seem like a wasteland at first, as the country's petroleum industry is based there; oil drills, pipelines, and storage barrels are scattered throughout the parched and barren landscape. But when you see the main beach, you understand why Máncora is a surfer's paradise: The water is warm and clean and filled with breaks to explore, and there are sunny skies overhead. After the morning session, surfers pile up at the Hotel del Wawa, which is a small hotel featuring Peruvian-Polynesian hangout decor—hammocks, bamboo nooks, and palm-shaded sun chairs. In the afternoon, surfers load into cars and troll other breaks along the coast, sometimes finding them in the funky ghost towns originally built by Americans in the 1940s for military or oil-drilling purposes.

The Mulanoviches can often be found in the evenings at the pyramidal surf shack belonging to José de Col, a pro surfer and architect. De Col was inspired by Mayan architecture when he designed this shack. He cooks up big Asian-Peruvian fusion dinners over a fire pit atop a rocky cliff with the surf rolling in below. The endless summer, as it turns out, is still going strong, if you know where to look.

ALAN FAENA

Alan Faena is the quintessential Gypset businessman. When he turned a reedy patch of neglected waterfront in Buenos Aires into a chic hotel and condominiums designed by Philippe Starck, he didn't just name it after of the nearest street or something that sounded Italian or French. He called it the Faena Hotel + Universe, which is definitely out there for the corporate world, but kind of cool if you know Faena and understand that he's not kidding about the "universe" part. Like dreamy utopians before him—Frank Lloyd Wright, Buckminster Fuller, and Frederick Kiesler, to name a few—Faena is interested in remaking the world into a groovier place. And if his utopia just so happens to make a handsome profit, so much the better.

Faena, who got his start as a fashion designer, generally dresses in some combination of white—white jeans, white trench coat, white cowboy hat, and, most important, hand-tooled leather cowboy boots from Mexico that he collects like a rapper might collect limited-edition sneakers. The effect is out of this world: Faena always looks as if he just stepped off a spaceship, fresh from some sort of decadent soiree in another galaxy. His personal commitment to far-out fashion makes his hotel project all the more impressive, considering that his first order of business was to make his investors feel comfortable about handing him hundreds of millions of redevelopment dollars.

In 2001, when Faena first got the idea to turn the run-down granaries and mills of Puerto Madero, the Buenos Aires port area, into a high-end property development, Argentina was in the midst of an economic collapse. The government was freezing bank accounts, the Argentine peso was severely devalued, and angry depositors were protesting in the streets—but Faena was unfazed. He sauntered into Puerto Madero with his crew of avant-garde artists, architects, and designers. Philippe Starck did his most unrestrained interiors to date: a belle epoque overhaul with unicorns and white chesterfields. British architect Norman Foster redesigned a former grain warehouse in the neighborhood to become apartments and the headquarters of Faena's Laboratory for Artistic Experimentation, a company created to provide entertainment and culture for the "universe." At last check, Cuban installation artist Wilfredo Prieto was filling one of the vast spaces with dried corn and a single, pecking chicken. "Every project we design we see as a work of art," Faena explains. "We are a group of artists merging our vision with reality."

When not in Buenos Aires, Faena can often be found on soulful treks—climbing to Peru's Machu Picchu, meditating at an ashram in India, or soaking in the hot-spring baths of a Japanese *ryokan*. I happened upon Faena a few years ago in José Ignacio, a little beach community in Uruguay about forty-five minutes up the coast from Punta del Este. I had been invited to a dinner party at his house through mutual friends, and when I drove down the long dirt driveway, the first thing I noticed was his garden. The shrubbery had been sculpted into surreal swirls resembling frosting on a birthday cake, as though a South American Edward Scissorhands had been let loose with his whimsical shears. On the lawn a bed of blooming yellow flowers encircled a serene stone deity. Faena had picked up the deity in India and positioned it with a commanding view of the Atlantic Ocean. And everywhere, there were rosebushes—more than three thousand on the property.

Faena's house appeared normal enough, a simple wooden structure painted sky blue with white trim that easily could have been found on Cape Cod or in the Hamptons. But inside, things began to reveal themselves as decidedly unconventional. The big main living room had colored stripes

Previous pages: Hotelier Alan Faena strikes a pose at his Buenos Aires hotel (above). Faena's gaucho and Hindi-inspired beach house in José Ignacio, Uruguay.

painted down the floor like flamboyant planks. Hindu deities cavorted on tapestries hung on the walls next to candelabras, a Buddha sat in lotus position on a shelf above the record collection, and a Virgin Mary stood on the mantel. The mash of references was difficult to decipher, and it wasn't going to get any easier when I found Faena. He was in the woods out back with some gauchos who were grilling steak over an *asada* pit. When I asked him whether he was Catholic, Hindu, or Buddhist, he just handed me a glass of wine and pointed at the stars.

Faena has the Gypset talent for finding a special place way ahead of the curve. When he first bought his house, José Ignacio was a quiet fishing village with just a few houses and miles of beach. Partyers went to Punta del Este, the sort of Monte Carlo of South America, with garish nightclubs and cocaine-culture high-rises: Peach-colored marble, brass fixtures, and tinted glass. In the past few years the Buenos Aires fashion crowd and their global counterparts have inched up the coast and are now firmly rooted in José Ignacio. In the summer months, from New Year's until late February, paparazzi camp out on the windswept beaches and in the evenings revelers peel around hunting down parties tucked away in hidden estancias. Yet José Ignacio is still incredibly charming. Architects from Buenos Aires have subtly tweaked the small, traditional-style homes, giving the sculpted straw roofs more pitch to tease the eyes, sleekening the earthy white adobe into geometric, modernist lines.

The day after the dinner party at Faena's, I decided to stop by unannounced. He wasn't home; his friends told me he was "out back" and motioned to the forest. Gamely, I trudged into the woods to find him, feeling a little like Sanger Rainsford in *The Most Dangerous Game*—the hunter becomes the hunted. I wandered the leafy paths for a while and eventually came upon a clearing. There was a bench that Faena must have set up for himself, so I sat down to rest. Stretching out before me was a secret panoramic view of the ocean, with boats and clouds moving like toys across the horizon. I never did find Faena, but I got the feeling that was the point.

ASHLEY BICKERTON

If tortured French colonial painter Paul Gauguin had possessed a punk-rock sense of humor and a short board, then he'd have a lot more in common with artist Ashley Bickerton than a fetish for the South Pacific. Once a massive art star in New York City, Bickerton has been in self-exile on the Indonesian isle of Bali for the past fifteen years. Like Gauguin, he paints beautiful, naked island girls. But in Bickerton's canvases the girls share the portrait with him, and he looks like a sex-crazed, beer-bloated expat, wearing a wild smile and board shorts, mixed-race babies crawling around his feet.

Above: Bickerton goes native in a hand-woven straw hat. *Right:* Playing the bemused expat in his still life *Extradition with Computer*, c-print in mother-of-pearl inlaid frame, 2006.

Dictionary
MOLOKAI: AN ISLAND IN TIME
VISIONS of AMERICA

Bickerton derives naughty pleasure from upsetting fragile expatriate fantasies, but this is a relatively new phase.

In the 1980s Bickerton was basking in art-world fame; he was selling work for six figures a pop through the Sonnabend Gallery and being feted by wealthy collectors, who picked up his large tabs at Barocco and Indochine. As part of the elite "Fab Four," along with Peter Halley, Jeff Koons, and Meyer Vaisman, he even had his own movement, Neo-Geo, short for Neo-Geometric Conceptualism. He grinned from the cover of *Artforum,* having had praise heaped upon him for his *Landscape #1,* which a critic described as a Judd-like wall work gone heavy metal—a high-tech, accessorized box labeled with the words "Season 87–88." A red LED tracked the work's changing value, starting at $25,000; it only went up" is how one art critic described it at the time.

Bickerton loved the ego boost, but he says living in New York "felt like being in a big, cold underground parking lot. It was gray and endless, like holding your breath in a dirty soup." So when the stock market bottomed out, along with the art market, in the late eighties, Bickerton did the proper nomadic thing and hit the road. Channeling his inner gypsy, he packed just two suitcases, one with clothes and the other with art supplies. His plan was to be transient, shacking up in various hotel rooms around the world and creating small works on paper that he could tote around easily in his dog-eared portfolio.

In reality, Bickerton was just reverting to the roving lifestyle of his youth. His father was a linguist and scholar of Creole whose career had kept the family moving around the world. They had hopped from the Caribbean islands to the jungles of South America to the Spanish Balearics. Bickerton was born along the way, in Barbados.

"I remember living in tents as a child and eating ants in my cornflakes," Bickerton recalls. When he was twelve, they moved to Honolulu, where he learned to surf in the balmy Waikiki swell. At an age when most kids were studying formal languages like French and Latin, Bickerton was speaking five varieties of pidgin English.

After abandoning the New York art world, Bickerton embarked on a new life of hotel room service and lavender hand soap. He headed to a group show in Brazil and soon found himself in the eastern state of Bahia in the remote fishing village of Trancoso. He moved into a small riverside mud hut that had spotty plumbing and electricity. The primitive lifestyle suited him, a vigilante type. Except it was nearly impossible to find art supplies. "I had to drive for an hour and a half through a jungle," he recalls, "take a ferry, and then drive some more, to a place where I could buy paintbrushes for children." He had to beg workers at the local hotel to use their fax machine and telephone. The art world was receding further into the ether, and he had started an affair with a woman who was dating one of the buddies of "the Colonel," a gun-happy local lawman. It seemed like a good time to skip town.

During his art-star days, Bickerton used to jet off to Bali for surf trips—and to be on the other side of the planet from New York. "It's one of the Shangri-las of surfing," he explains. "A mythical land of the perfect life, full of temples, long waves, and mystical reefs."

Bickerton, his Brazilian girlfriend in tow, found a typical expat home on the outskirts of Basangkasa by the paddy fields in Bali, and set about transforming it into a "florid colonial fantasy," as he describes it, one outfitted with spears, paddles, canoes, a giant water buffalo skull with horns, candleholders, and more daybeds than a Miami nightclub. (He eventually split with the Brazilian and is now married to an Indonesian woman.) "Dream architecture" is Bickerton's term for the homes expats in Indonesia erect—tropical San Simone's loaded with clichés and butchered cultural references. Inspired by Salvador Dalí's piecemeal approach to erecting his house in Figueres, Spain, Bickerton over time added on guest rooms, chill-out nooks, and decks. He also built a surf perch he called Monkey Rock in Padang Pagang overlooking the legendary Indian ocean break. As Gauguin wrote in the 1890s to his wife, who was suffering in Denmark while he was in Tahiti: "You say that I am wrong for staying away too long from the center of the art world. . . . The center of my art world is in my head, not anywhere else."

Bickerton's head was becoming more and more immersed in both the beauty and the crassness of Bali. At first he tried to resist the urge to become "one of those schmaltzy, kitschy fantasists who want to do pastels of island charm," he says. He tried to seal himself away in a New York City–style white cubed concrete studio, but he was helpless against the pervasive touristy forces around him. Soon his work had changed from slick and urban to cracked-out tropical; one piece featured a topless local girl wearing a shell-and-flower anklet snuggling on a daybed with a blue-painted gringo in a sarong, both gazing out at a picture-perfect sea. "Gauguin was always the white elephant in the room that I had to tiptoe around," Bickerton says. "So finally I thought, why not just deal with it? Not only deal with it, but dive in and play with it."

Bickerton is just getting started. He's plotting his own Valhalla in the less developed southern part of the island on the Bukit peninsula, a paradise that will trump all of the giant McFantasy palaces down there. He is now featured in Lonely Planet's Bali guide, making him his own best muse and worst fear: A tourist attraction. The new house will be his most ambitious artwork yet. "It'll be vaguely South Seas," he "says. "Like a B-grade film where they don't know the difference between hula dancers giving leis and doing the limbo. All mixed up."

"IF TORTURED FRENCH COLONIAL PAINTER PAUL GAUGUIN HAD A PUNK-ROCK SENSE OF HUMOR AND A SHORT BOARD THAN HE'D HAVE A LOT MORE IN COMMON WITH ARTIST ASHLEY BICKERTON THAN A FETISH FOR THE SOUTH PACIFIC."

Bickerton hard at work in his art studio in Basangkasa, Bali.

Previous page: Bickerton's surf clubhouse Monkey Rock, built into the hills overlooking Padang Padang, the legendary Indian Ocean break.

HOME
NOW

CREDITS

p. 4: © Anne Menke; p. 6: © Hilary Walsh; p. 9, clockwise from top left: © Gordon Chaplin, © Gordon Chaplin, © Deborah Schoeneman, © Gordon Chaplin, © Kim Milliken, © Mareen Fischinger, © Julia Chaplin; p. 11: © Holly Chaplin; p. 12, 14, 15: © Anne Menke; p. 16-17: © Paul Almasy/Corbis; p. 19, clockwise from top left: © Rue des Archives/The Granger Collection, © Rue des Archives/The Granger Collection, © Popperfoto/Getty Images, © Thierry Rajic, © Haillot/Apis/Sygma/Corbis; p. 20-21: © Mr. Henk; p. 23: © 2008, Lucien Clergue; p. 24: © Peter Knapp/Scoop; p. 26: © All rights reserved; p. 28: © James Waddell; p. 29: *Vogue*/Condé Nast Archives © Condé Nast Publications; p. 32, clockwise from top left: © Everett Collection, © Evening Standard/Hulton Archive/Getty Images, © Hulton Archive/Getty Images, © Francisco Hidalgo/Top-Rapho/Eyedea, © Henry Diltz/Corbis; p. 34: © Oberto Gili; p. 35, 36, 38-39, 40: *Vogue*/Condé Nast Archives © Condé Nast Publications; p. 42: © Zuma Press; p. 43, clockwise from left: © Rue des Archives/The Granger Collection, © Everett Collection, © Princes Films/The Kobal Collection, © Jet Films/The Kobal Collection; p. 45: © Everett Collection; p. 46, 47: *Vogue*/Condé Nast Archives © Condé Nast Publications; p. 48-49: © Thomas Dorn; p. 52: © The Gallery Collection/Corbis; p. 55, 56: © Bettmann/Corbis; p. 57: Courtesy Tareq Rajab Museum, Kuwait; p. 59: © Rue des Archives/The Granger Collection; p. 62: © The State Hermitage Museum, St. Petersburg/The Bridgeman Art Library; p. 63: © Rue des Archives/The Granger Collection; p. 65: © Popperfoto/Getty Images; p. 67: © Bettmann/Corbis; p. 69: © Roger Viollet/Getty Images; p. 70: © Rue des Archives/The Granger Collection; p. 71: © Hulton Archive/Getty Images; p. 73: © Angelo Hornak/Corbis; p. 74: © Allen Ginsberg/Corbis; p. 77: © Fred W. McDarrah/Getty Images; p. 78: Reprinted by permission of SLL/Sterling Lord Literistic, Inc. Copyright by Jack Kerouac, Image courtesy The New York Public Library; p. 79, clockwise from top left: © Herbert List/Magnum Photos, © Allen Ginsberg/Corbis, © Allen Ginsberg/Corbis, © Jan Butchofsky-Houser/Corbis, © James Burke/Time Life Pictures/Getty Images, © Silvia Otte/Photonica/Getty Images; p. 82: © Sasha Eisenman/Trunk Archives; p. 85: Courtesy Condé Nast Publications; p. 88: © Benoît Peverelli; p. 89: © Simon Upton/The Interior Archive; p. 90-91: © Roger Wood/Corbis; p. 94: © Simon Upton/The Interior Archive; p. 95: © Benoît Peverelli; p. 96, 97, 98, 99: © Anne Menke; p. 102, 103, 104, 105: © James Merrell; p. 108, 109, 111, 112, 113: © Anne Menke; p. 117: © Sebastian Mlynarski/Getty Images; p. 120, 121, 122-123: © Venetia Dearden; p. 127, 129: © Henry Bourne/Trunk Archives; p. 130, 131: Courtesy Andrea Zittel; p. 134, 135, 136-137, 138: Photo by Simon Douglas-Dufresne, courtesy Carolyn Roumeguere collection; p. 139: © Elizabeth Gilbert; p. 142, 143: © Dan Busta; p. 144: © José de Col; p. 145: © Dan Busta; p. 148: Courtesy Alan Faena Group; p. 149: © Ximena Caminos; p. 152, 153, 154, 157: Courtesy Ashley Bickerton; p. 158: © Julia Chaplin. Gypset Type embellishments: © Cyrene Mary.

A work of art by Jack Pierson, made from old roadside letters in Joshua Tree, California.

ACKNOWLEDGMENTS

The author wishes to thank the following people for their contributions to the book: My parents, Gordon and Holly, for their love, support and commitment to the lifestyle; Gypsetters extraordinaire Garth Murphy and Euva Anderson, for the inspiration and the surf; and la familia: Diana, Avery, Eli, Susie, Sarah, and Rosie Chaplin.

My Gypset muses: Nathalie and Laurence Mignot, Ines Mulanovich, Maia Norman, Andrea Zittel, Carolyn Roumeguere, Peter Beard, Basile, Catrine and Eric, and Claudius of Paris. My travel editors: Alison Humes, Stuart Emmrich, Mary Billard, Denny Lee, and Miranda Purves. Gypset support: Sia Michel, Jamie Brisick, Tanya Selvaratnum, Deborah Schoeneman, Zeina Durra, Esther Kremer, Perrine Scherrer, and Martine Assouline. Special thanks to Adam Fisher for his expert and generous editing. And Jason Miller, friend and confidant to the Gypset, and much more. And to all my friends who shared their time, advice, and encouragement. XO.

The editor wishes to thank all the Gypsetters who are profiled in this book:
Devendra Banhart, Ashley Bickerton, Consuelo Castiglioni, Alan Faena, Sean Gullette and Yto Barrada, Damien Hirst and Maia Norman, Jade Jagger, Nicolas Malleville, the Mignot sisters, the Mulanovich family, Carolyn Roumeguere, Alice Temperley, and Andrea Zittel.

The editor also would like to thank all the photographers, particularly Henry Bourne, Dan Busta, Ximena Caminos, Lucien Clergue, Venetia Dearden, Thomas Dorn, Sasha Eisenman, Elizabeth Gilbert, Oberto Gili, Mr. Henk, Peter Knapp, Anne Menke, James Merrell, Benoît Peverelli, Thierry Rajic, Simon Upton, James Waddell, Hilary Walsh.

A thank you also to all those who participated in the pictorial realization of this work: Djilali Boubekeur (Scoop), Scarlett Chang (Alice Temperley office), Géraldine Chanut (Lucien Clergue), Chico and The Gipsy Kings, José de Col, Veronique Colaprete (The Kobal Collection), Céline Couturier (Figure), Silvana Davanzo (Eyedea), Maggie Downing and Silka Quintero (The Granger Collection), Tania Fernández (Trunk Archives), Robert Guinsler (SLL), Libby Haan (Karla Otto, Inc.), Amanda Harding (Purple PR), Karen Howes (The Interior Archive), Alison J. Rigney (Everett Collection), Dilcia Johnson (Corbis), Malick Kane (Getty Images), Thomas Lisanti (New York Public Library), Dawn Lucas, Leigh Montville, Elyce Tetorka and Shawn Waldron (Condé Nast Publications), Maria Murguia (Bridgeman Art Library), Trish Murphy (Zuma Press), Mohammad Safdar (Tareq Rajab Museum, Kuwait), Angelika Saint-Aignan (Anne Menke Studios, LLC), Michael Shulman (Magnum Photos), and Barbara von Schreiber.